SPORT
IMAGES

SPORT IMAGES, 13291 FALCON POINT PLACE, TRUCKEE, CALIFORNIA 96161 USA TELEPHONE: 530-582-4579

PRINTED IN CHINA

ISBN 0-9618712-0-2

THE GOLF COURSES OF
THE MONTEREY PENINSULA

A SPORT IMAGES BOOK BY UDO MACHAT
Text by CAL BROWN

Foreword by Jack Whitaker

SPORT IMAGES, TRUCKEE, CALIFORNIA, USA

To Sandy Tatum and Ken Venturi,
each of whom has given so much to the game,
and to this book.

Foreword

WE WILL KNOW OUR CIVILIZA-
tion is doomed when they build the first
indoor golf course. In baseball and football,
we have seen how the insensitive invasion
of artificial turf and domed stadia has
struck at the very spirit of these two pas-
times. At the Olympic Games in Calgary,
most events were contested on artificial
surfaces and three of the most popular
attractions were played indoors, thus pointing the way to the day when Miami can
host the winter games. Yes, the day of arti-
ficially controlled sports environments is
here. So far, golf has been able to withstand
this onslaught.

The Great Game can adapt to the
two-piece ball, graphite shafts and square
grooves, but it would wither and die
indoors, and so would those noble ideals of
loving nature, fresh air, wind and rain.

One of golf's greatest gifts is to push our
noses into nature, to make us aware of sky
and mountain, tree and stream, ocean and
beach, flora and fauna.

There are so many truly lovely places
to play golf in the world that few of us
would have the heart to name a favorite.
Those that appeal to us most are those that
appear most natural, those that seem to
have been created just for golf. The Monterey Peninsula is of that company. There
are other peninsulas that are richer, more
populated, more strategically situated than
this sliver of the American continent, but
none can surpass the beauty that is
Monterey.

Its old California history mingles easily
with John Steinbeck's Cannery Row and
the prudent town of Pacific Grove. The
past moves softly through the streets of

Carmel, a town saved from terminal quaintness by the great western ocean that pounds itself against Carmel's doorstep, slinging great white spume into the air.

The mists and fogs that swirl among the stately pines and through the village streets whisper of mystery and romance, and have lured writers and artists to make their homes here for more than a hundred years. Since the golfer is not far removed from a writer or an artist, it was inevitable that golf and the Monterey Peninsula would meet and produce a world of harmony and delight. It is a world that is portrayed with much delight and beauty in this book, which, as it happens, is a collaboration between a writer, Cal Brown, and an artist, Udo Machat, who share an abiding affection for the Great Game and for one of its grandest settings.

On a peninsula so blest by nature, fate also was kind in its choice of the men who would guide its destiny and build its golf courses. It is remarkable that they were able to keep their minds on their business.

For several years I was assigned the seventeenth hole at Pebble Beach during the telecasts of the Bing Crosby Tournament. Time and again I would find my mind and eyes wandering away to the hills beyond Carmel, so reminiscent of the glens of Scotland, the light diffusing the colors to soft purples and browns. Then, wrenching myself back to the business at hand, I would be diverted again by a sea otter frisking gaily on his back, lunching on a local delicacy. And to look across the bay to the Mission at Carmel where Junipero Serra is buried is to be transported far away from the problems of an errant tee shot or a nasty chip shot at that dramatic par three hole.

Cal Brown has caught the character and personality of these courses with affection and the wonder and the insight they and their creators deserve. The photographs by Udo Machat are riveting and seductive, making us want to call for a tee time right away. With this book, the Monterey Peninsula becomes a moveable feast.

There is no such thing as an ugly golf course. Some are just prettier than others. That is especially true on the Monterey Peninsula. Bobby Jones once said that if he could play only one golf course, it would be the Old Course at St. Andrews. I can't argue with that. But if eternity should find me some misty morning on the Seventeen Mile Drive, my Sunday bag over my shoulder, on the way to the first tee at Pebble or Spyglass or Cypress, I will not be unhappy. Neither will Cal Brown nor will Udo Machat.

And, neither will you.

JACK WHITAKER

Bridgehampton, New York
June 1988

Contents

Introduction

BEHIND EVERY GREAT MAN, it used to be said, there is a great woman. Although this is no longer a fashionable notion, one is tempted to draw such a connection between Sam Morse and Mother Nature. Metaphorically, of course.

Samuel Finley Brown Morse was a Massachusetts boy who made good. He became an All America fullback at Yale, went west to seek his fortune and found it. With the help of Yale contacts, he landed a job with the Pacific Improvement Company, a holding company containing the accumulated spoils of California railroad tycoons Leland Stanford, Charles Crocker, Mark Hopkins and Collis P. Huntington. After managing a subsidiary, Morse was put in charge of liquidating the company's assets, which included seven thousand acres on the Monterey Peninsula, fifty-three hundred of which Morse wanted for himself. In 1915, with the help of a banker friend, he got them. The property included the once-famous but now broken-down Del Monte Hotel. Morse dreamed of a world-class luxury resort and spent the next fifty years achieving it. He made all the rules and most of the decisions with a wily, autocratic style that earned him the unofficial title of the Duke of Monterey. Morse died in 1969 at the age of eighty-three. He left an extraordinary example of how to behave when the object is to create and nurture a resort development of enduring character, an example that often goes unnoticed. Morse was a hard-headed, hard-boiled Yankee, yet he took care not to trample upon nature because he clearly understood the importance of the environment to the fulfillment of his vision. The greatest satis-

faction of these courses is that they engage us fully in the natural world about us, for which we can thank Morse and the gifted golf architects who so obviously crafted their courses to complement the works of Mother Nature, rather than tame them.

The golf courses here present so many powerful images that one could easily fill a book double or triple the size of this one. The golf course photographs were taken by Udo Machat, who also designed the book and was the guiding force behind the project. The writer was along for the ride, using Machat's stunning photographic portraits as a centerpiece, taking on bits of story to give the pictures some context.

A word about definitions. The Monterey Peninsula area includes many more golf courses, from the much-admired tests at Fort Ord to the splendid layouts of Carmel Valley. To have included these would have more than doubled the size of the book. Early on, it was clear that if the project were to be manageable, a rather strict geographical limit would have to be drawn. And so it was, on a line running through the base of the peninsula from the southern end of the Seventeen Mile Drive northeast to Fisherman's Wharf in Monterey.

In glancing through the book, I am struck by the sunny disposition of most of the photographs. One depends upon good sunlight to show the features of a golf course, and therefore you will not sense one of the overpowering influences of playing golf on the Monterey Peninsula. It is weather, "lots of it," as Bing Crosby once understated. When the skies darken and the wind howls, it can be a fearsome place. There is no certainty to the weather either. The place can be calm and beautiful in December or February, or cold and fierce in July, the rain slicing diagonally across the course and stabbing into every exposed pore. In a gale one wants a stout heart, and, as Jackie Burke once observed, fat caddies are in great demand. Once or twice during the Bing Crosby Tournament it has been so cold that the courses have become frozen and slabs of ice have blown down the fairway, and Cary Middlecoff was once moved to wonder if anyone had ever played casual ice.

Well, you will have to see it for yourself. That so many extraordinary golf courses should have arisen in the same place is among the wonders of golf. There is a temptation to write everything there is to know about each of them, but that would deprive you of the pleasure of discovering them for yourself, and besides I'm not up to the task. The beauty of this book is in its photographs. For some, they will be a tantalizing introduction to these incomparable courses; for others, a reminder of adventures past. If you detect a tone of enthusiasm in the text, it is quite real, but I offer no apology for this because it goes with the place.

Sam Morse knew this from his first moment there. In his memoirs, he recalls the day in 1908, and his reaction: "It had an electrifying effect on me. I don't know of any place with which to compare it. It makes you want to run and shout. It is full of the joy of living."

And still is.

CAL BROWN

Wayland, Massachusetts
July 1988

Pebble Beach Golf Links

At its most elemental, golf is a form of combat, man against nature, in which man seeks the most direct, most efficient and sometimes the most elegant path to an objective. Paradoxically, before we can tame the terrors of nature and terrain we first must tame the demons of ego, nerves, bravado, fear and doubt, or, as Old Finley Peter Dunne once wrote, "It is the kind of game that you play with your own worst enemy; which is yourself."

Small wonder, then, that the gratifications of the game are most keenly felt where the natural setting is most dramatic and ominous, where nature exhibits herself most spectacularly. It does not always follow that the most majestic setting produces the most challenging golf, but when they coincide, as they do at Pebble Beach, who but the terminally numb can resist?

The scenery alone, a setting that Pat Ward-Thomas, the respected British golf essayist, called the noblest in golf, would be enough to place Pebble Beach in a special rank among the world's courses. Its fairways slope gently toward Carmel Bay on the southern flank of the Monterey Peninsula, nearly half of the holes running along the jagged, ocean-whipped cliffs that supply so much grandeur and menace of the course. Tall Monterey pines form a backdrop for The Lodge and the elegant homesites that flank the northern borders of the course. The ocean panorama is visible even from the inland holes, a promise and a reminder of imagined glories. Below the cliffs, when the tide is out, people stroll the beach, leopard seals and sea lions nest and bark, otters play in the surf and cormorants dive swiftly from the sky for fish. At dusk, when the light has all but faded and you gaze from The Lodge across the ghostly lawn of the eighteenth fairway, the sea wind fills the nostrils with a whiff of brine

and cooling turf and you wonder if there is another place on earth quite like it.

One cannot imagine that any developer of today would have the audacity to commit such priceless terrain to a golf course, but Samuel Morse was not without audacity and certainly not an ordinary man. Morse had acquired fifty-three hundred acres on the Monterey Peninsula, including Pebble Beach, in 1915, and had dreams of creating a world-class resort and residential enclave. Golf was the coming thing. Francis Ouimet, an unheralded Massachusetts caddie, had won the United States Open just two years before, the first authentic American golf hero, and the game was becoming a hugely popular pastime. It did not escape Morse's notice that it was attracting an affluent and sporty segment of society. As he surveyed his new domain, Morse found that the meadowland sloping down to the ocean at Pebble Beach, which were being used for picnics and grazing sheep, had been plotted in eighty-foot lots for future residential development. He must have felt that there was plenty of shoreline and other land for that sort of thing, and when he decided to place the golf course on its present site, the character and stature of

Pebble Beach was almost certainly settled. The golf course could hardly be less spectacular than the terrain it would occupy.

Morse knew little about golf but knew enough to consult those who did. To design the course, he chose Jack Neville, and to assist him, Douglas Grant. Both were well-known amateur players and each had won the California Amateur Championship; Neville three times. While some of the inland holes, particularly at the beginning, emerged with no special distinction, neither were they without golfing merit, and when they got to the ocean, Neville and Grant obviously knew what to do.

"It was all there in plain sight," Neville said years later. "The big idea was to get in as many holes as possible along the bay. It took a little imagination, but not much. Years before it was built I could see Pebble Beach as a golf links. Nature had intended that it be nothing else."

Most of the fine players of the day had to be masterful shotmakers because of the equipment with which they played and the generally ragged condition of the golf courses. Neville and Grant were no exceptions. They built smallish greens, averaging no more than thirty-five hundred to four thousand

The real glory of Pebble Beach begins at the long sixth,
which surmounts an imposing headland with
steep cliffs falling away on the right.

square feet in area, that leave no doubt as to what they intended. By today's standards these greens are tiny, but if weather and terrain are the soul of this course these little greens are its heart; they will flat make you hit some golf shots. The greens are well protected by bunkers, mounds, gulleys and tall grasses like kikuyu, a clinging and distinctly distasteful growth that has all the appeal of nesting tarantulas.

There are cross-hazards scattered about the course, a treatment that is no longer in fashion; but most of these are quite natural. Neville and Grant must have understood that a fabricated hole cannot compete in our affections with a natural one, because Pebble Beach has a very natural, in some cases almost ungainly look. Our attraction to natural obstacles is instinctive and compelling, which is why so many of our grandest golf courses, from the Old Course at St. Andrews to Ballybunion to Pine Valley, arise in terrain where the scale of nature and its hazards are grandest. There are few places where the scale of nature is grander than at Pebble Beach, and when we come to the ocean holes we come to the real glory and agony of this course.

It begins at the sixth hole, a par five that climbs awkwardly

The mischievous seventh, a tiny par three, is circled by bunkers, rocks and the ocean.
It clings perilously to the edge of the headland, brutally exposed to the elements
that make it a hair-raising test of judgment and courage.

upward onto an imposing headland with sheer cliffs falling fifty feet into Stillwater Cove. Surmounting the hill, the hole trails off in the distance to the point of the head-land completely exposed to the weather and the wind. It is only a foretaste of what is to come, for this is the easiest of the ocean holes.

The seventh is a mischievous piece of work that can be attrib-uted to either genius or blind luck, both of which are needed to play the hole. It is a tiny par three of no more than 110 yards that falls twenty feet from an elevated tee to a speck of green that is encircled by bunkers, rocks and the ocean. On a calm day it is no more than a three-quarters pitch shot. You can almost roll the ball down the hill onto the green, provided you can dodge the bunkers. When the wind is in your face, as it often is, you may need to hit a full five-iron. During the Bing Crosby Tourna-ment one year, Ken Venturi hit a four-iron here into a near gale-force wind, and in similar condi-tions during the Crosby the fine professional from Bel Air, Eddie Merrins, scored a hole in one with a three-iron. It is almost as bad when the wind is behind, because the only hope is to keep the ball low, a tricky business, or pop the ball in the air with a sand wedge

and pray. Ernie Vossler, a man of uncommon intelligence and one of the finest strikers of his day, had the wit to use his putter from the tee during a particularly hard blow, rolling the ball deliberately into a bunker, reasoning that the short sand shot was a better deal than what might happen if he put the ball in the air. In a strong wind, it is sometimes hard to believe what you need to hit in order to reach the green, but this little hole is a wonderful and hair-raising test of judgment and courage.

The eighth hole is one of the wonders of golf and begins a stretch of consecutive par fours along the ocean cliffs that are unmatched for their pure difficulty and splendor. The eighth travels back over the headland, with cliffs and ocean on the right, over a hump that forces a blind tee shot and then swerves dramatically to the right around a chasm filled with jagged rocks and the rolling ocean to a green that sets into the cliffside some 430 yards away. The idea is to position the drive close enough to the cliff that you will have a medium to long iron approach across the chasm; but this takes some doing, especially since the tee shot is blind. For the cautious golfer who drives to the left, it is quite possible to hit a long tee shot

and, because of the sharp angle to the hole, have a full wood to the green. Whatever its length, that second shot is about as good as the game ever gets, a classic example of heroic design. Any stroke that falls short or wavers a shade to the right of the green will be consumed by the rocks or the ocean. One imagines that it might be safer to play long or to the left of the green, but one reckons without the cheer-ful mind of Alister MacKenzie. Several years after Pebble Beach opened, while MacKenzie and his partner Robert Hunter were work-ing on Cypress Point, they were brought in to redesign the eighth and thirteenth greens. At the eighth, they built a small green that slopes toward the ocean; it is the fastest on the course. You would scarcely believe the ease with which a gentle pitch from behind or from the left of the green will skitter across the putting surface and dis-appear over the cliff. So this is not a hole to play too carefully, nor was it made for the fainthearted. Few shots in golf set the challenge with such breath-taking clarity and, once you have pictured the shot in your imagination, nothing can match the arching satisfaction of pulling it off. If the eighth is a wonder, then the ninth is a terror—magnificent, awesome, beautiful,

The eighth hole, shown on pages 22-23 is among the wonders of golf; a classic example of heroic design that
plays from the immense cliff in the background across the yawning chasm to the green in the foreground.
That second shot, shown above as the golfer sees it, is about as good as the game ever gets.

yes, but a terror nonetheless. It runs straight along the cliff for 464 yards, with the fairway tilting toward the ocean on the right, and narrows onto a scene that can be described, with some justification, as one of golf's nastiest arrangements. The green rests somewhat uneasily on the edge of the cliff that curls around its right and rear edges. To the left is a large mound that tumbles across the front of the green and, just as it ends, some silly ass has placed a bunker with a very sharp face on the precise line on which any sensible person would aim an approach shot. Since the fairway slants to the ocean, one needn't be told to avoid the right side of the hole. And this sets up a ticklish problem here because, except for a personage, Moses perhaps, with some experience at parting the waters, the hole was not built to be played from the left side. One then would face an approach of two hundred yards or more, across that nasty business on the left of the green, all the while aiming pretty much at the ocean. No thanks, but maybe five is not a bad score on this hole. Cary Middlecoff says that the eighth and ninth holes at Pebble Beach are "the two hardest consecutive holes in golf. Your heart is in your mouth. And if you can play eight,

nine and ten in one over par, you feel like you've whipped the field."

The tenth is a shorter version of the ninth, but only slightly shorter, and is just as treacherous because the fairway tilts more sharply toward the ocean. Most tee shots hit to the middle of the fairway just bound away to the right and over the cliff. The green is perched even more precariously over the cliffs than is the ninth, and it is smaller. The approach is a glorious and testing shot, even for long hitters who are going in with short irons. It is a mark of the designers' understanding of the game and their perspective on its playing values that the greens at both nine and ten have been left sufficiently open in front to permit a running approach shot. This is an element of skill that is, regrettably, disappearing from American golf and it is comforting that this element of the game will survive in America so long as courses like Pebble Beach endure. At this point of the golf course, where the holes are most exposed to the fierce winds, the running shot is an appropriate and most welcome option.

Beginning at the eleventh, the course moves inland and eases somewhat. The relief is temporary, though, since several of these inland holes can easily put you in a

serious mood. The thirteenth, for example, is an uphill par four with out-of-bounds on the right and a fairway that tilts left. The green tilts to the left, too, and there is a nifty bunker guarding the approach shot on this vastly underrated hole. The fourteenth is the longest, at 565 yards, and in many ways the most testing hole on the course. It rises gradually in a giant sweep around to the right, where the fairway is flanked by trees and out-of-bounds, and as you clamber forward you are pounding the ball uphill with all the force and skill you can muster. The green is elevated and partially hidden by an enormous bunker whose banks are infested with thick colonies of kikuyu grass, into which balls have been known to disappear without a trace, so this is one place on the course where it would be useful to produce a shot with a nice, high, safe trajectory. And try not to land in the roller-coaster swale at the front of the green, as Danny Edwards did during the 1977 PGA Tournament, a point from which he, sadly, took six putts.

The course heads back toward the ocean at the sixteenth, a shortish par four that is an interesting transition hole because it provides a reasonable birdie chance with a hint of trouble. The green tilts

The majestic stretch of oceanside par fours continues with the ninth and tenth holes,
shown above and also on pages 30—31. Their fairways eaten away by the relentless forces of nature,
this is as beautiful a setting for terror as a golfer could want.

invitingly toward the fairway, nestled in a lovely copse of pine and cypress beyond a shallow ravine. The real trouble, though, is behind the green. One would not favor one's recovery chances from the mounds, bushes and thick grasses that lurk there.

The power of the finishing holes is commonly held to be a decisive factor in assessing the merits of a golf course, particularly those of championship caliber, and nowhere in golf is the finish more powerful than at Pebble Beach. The seventeenth and eighteenth are holes that separately fairly crackle with excitement and together form one of the memorable climaxes in golf.

The seventeenth is a one-shotter of robust proportions, fraught with peril, with a boundless potential for inflicting the most exquisite torture, or the most irrepressible glee. The hole points directly at the ocean, which is close enough to reach on the left and behind the green. The seventeenth was designed for a long iron and can be played from 170 to 218 yards, depending on wind conditions. Its most distinctive feature is a wide, shallow green that is pinched in the middle. This hourglass shape provides two distinct target areas, with a ridge running between them. The right side of the

green is open in front; the rest is surrounded by bunkers. It matters a great deal where the flagstick is placed because it changes the strategy of the hole and because, to avoid embarrassment, a golfer should play the ball to the same side of the green. Many a pilgrim has been observed putting helplessly from one end of the green to the other, through the rough that pinches in at the neck of the hourglass, in a melancholy attempt to reach the hole one hundred feet away. He might have preferred the bunker.

The charm of golf is that for every thousand miserable shots there is the odd stroke of genius, for every hopeless predicament there is the chance for redemption. One such moment occurred during the 1951 Bing Crosby Tournament when Dutch Harrison and his partner, Phil Harris, came to this hole with a chance to win the tournament. Harrison was about as good a player as there was in those days and he hit a four-wood into a stiff wind, but he hit it too hard and over the green it went. Harris half-sculled a driver onto the right side of the green. With the flagstick on the other end of the green, and Dutch in the hole in five strokes, Harris lined up his sixty-footer over the fringe and snaked it into

The eighteenth green is guarded on the right by a rather large Monterey pine, forcing the golfer to play the second shot as close to the water as he dares.

the hole for a natural two, a net one with handicap. They won the tournament, and for the rest of the day every time the story was repeated the putt got longer. That night at the awards dinner Harris was asked if it was true that the putt had traveled one hundred feet. Phil grinned and said, "Hell, it broke that much."

The seventeenth has been the scene of both triumph and disaster involving some of our greatest players. Who can forget 1982, when Tom Watson played one of the most sensational shots in history here to steal the U.S. Open Championship from Jack Nicklaus? Watson drove into the rough near the left edge of the green and had to play the next stroke downhill across a green that registered about twenty-three on the the Stimp Meter. There wasn't the remotest chance that he could stop the ball close to the hole, and a bogey would surely cost him the tournament. Unbelievably, Watson chipped the ball into the hole to beat Nicklaus by a stroke. "I couldn't have written the script better," Watson says today. "It was the championship I most wanted to win, on one of my favorite golf courses." Nicklaus himself had played a mighty stroke at the seventeenth when he won the U.S.

Open a decade earlier. Needing a par to hold off challengers, Nicklaus played a one-iron into the wind that never wavered from the flagstick, catching it on the fly and dropping inches away for an eventual birdie that helped him earn his third Open title. On another occasion, Arnold Palmer was not so fortunate. It was during the Crosby Tournament one year that Arnold missed the green badly and wound up among the rocks along the beach. The adventure cost him several strokes and consumed about twenty minutes of television time as Palmer watched his ball wash back and forth in the surf. It was a predicament that Jimmy Demaret could not resist. "What choice does he have? His nearest drop is Hawaii," Demaret advised the television audience. The eighteenth hole is a magnificent brute, stretching 548 yards between the ocean on the left and out-of-bounds on the right, curving gently to the left near the green, which sits close to the beach. Pat Ward-Thomas is not alone in claiming that it has no parallel as a long finishing hole. "Yeah, it has finished a lot of people," is the way one local wag puts it. It is a legitimate three-shot hole, not often reached in two, although Roberto De Vicenzo, the powerful Argentinian, managed this feat in

Among the inland holes, not often seen by non-golfers, are the twelfth, at right, a longish par three with its bunker covering the front and a putting surface that is hard to hold.

The fourteeth, above, with an elevated green half-hidden by the yawning bunker with its thick lip of kikuyu grass.

1961, an accomplishment rare enough that old-timers still remember it. The hole starts from a small nob that juts into the bay, giving the tee shot an angle over the edge of the cliff; two large pines provide a target in the right side of the fairway. A daring player might play for the left side of the fairway because the approach to the green is much easier from there, but the risk is high. A tall pine and bunkers guard the right side of the green, making the approach from that side much less attractive than it might seem. Ken Venturi says the eighteenth cannot be played timidly, an insight that is valuable but not very reassuring. The unrelenting pressure of the rocks and ocean, in a setting of such overpowering beauty, tends to induce the forced and awkward swing and sometimes leads players to adopt unusual playing methods. Many recall watching when Hale Irwin hit a screaming drive down the edge of the ocean, hoping of but not getting his accustomed fade. His horror turned to elation as the ball balanced off a rock and bounded into the fairway. All's well that ends well. "I don't see how you could make a hole that's any better," says Middlecoff. "It's just hard as the dickens. And I guess you'd have to say it's exciting because if

you make the slightest mistake, it'll just kill you. But, if the good Lord didn't want golf to be an exciting game, He wouldn't have given us Pebble Beach."

The course can be cruel to the unprepared or the unsteady hand. Bob Hope calls it Alcatraz with grass. Pebble Beach is, without doubt, a man-sized golf course that appeals to the healthy golfing appetite. Nicklaus has said that he prefers it to all others. "If I had only one more round to play, I would play it at Pebble Beach," he has said. "I can't imagine anyone creating a finer all-around test of golf in a more sensational setting. I've loved it since the first time I saw it." That would have been the 1961 U.S. Amateur, which Nicklaus won. Venturi, who won two California State Amateur Championships here and the Crosby once, believes that Pebble Beach is the greatest match-play course in the world. "It presents so many options for gambling or playing safe," he says. In the 1956 final, Venturi was two down to Bud Taylor going to the fifth hole, and made eight consecutive threes to win the match, two and one, a phenomenal stretch of scoring that lends some credence to his claim. Venturi recalls playing in weather "so bad the birds had to walk." In

The wide, shallow green at the seventeenth is beset by bunkers and pinched in the middle. An intimidating presence surrounded by stark beauty.

1960, when he won the Crosby, the wind was blowing the balls off the tees. "I was last off, leading the tournament by two stokes. I shot 77, and won by three. On the ninth hole, 450 yards, I hit a driver, a three-wood and a hard six-iron. I was just glad to get there," Venturi says.

Ed Sneed, whose graceful swing is accompanied by a thoughtful and analytic mind, explains why Pebble Beach is so well regarded by the game's best players. "Architecturally, Pebble Beach is one of the best we play on tour because of the mix and balance of shots it requires. It's not just that the shots look different, but rather that the shot values are varied and balanced among short, medium and long irons."

As a matter of historical interest, it should be noted that Pebble Beach owes much of its reputation to a character named H. Chandler Egan, who made significant changes to the course in the late 1920s. Chandler Egan was a Chicago blue-blood who had won two U.S. Amateur Championships, in 1905 and 1906, and later had moved to Oregon where he became a gentleman apple farmer and pursued his interest in golf course design. Morse brought in Egan in hopes of strengthening Pebble

Beach for the 1929 U.S. Amateur, the first national championship held in the West. The original course, which had opened in 1919, had been laid out by Neville and Grant as a par 74, and it covered 6,314 yards. Egan made major changes at eight holes, remodeled a number of greens and recast many of the greenside bunkers. At the ninth, a hole where Walter Hagen had struck a perfect drive of three hundred yards only to see it trickle into the ocean, Egan moved back the tee some thirty yards to its present location. But his greatest contribution came at the eighteenth, which Neville and Grant had designed as a par four of 379 yards. He moved the tee from the flat lawn onto the promontory where it now sits, adding 169 yards and bringing the full sweep of the ocean into view. It was a nice finishing hole, but Egan made it a great one.

Of all the natural hazards at Pebble Beach, weather is the most imposing and unpredictable. The Crosby Tournament, now the AT&T Pebble Beach National Pro-Am, is held in late January and is normally played in wet weather. The course is shortened out of consideration for the amateurs and, perhaps, the reputations of the professionals. Players have developed

The Peter Hay course, named after the Scotsman who served many years as the head professional at Pebble Beach, is a pleasntly diverting par three course within steps of The Lodge; a convenient place to warm up the short game.

ingenious ways to cope with the cold and rain. Phil Harris carried a bagful of mini-liquor bottles, the kind you find on airplanes. He called them "hand-warmers," and used them frequently. So did his caddie, a splendid character named Scorpy Doyle. One bitter morning, after liberally "warming up," Harris took a bleary swipe at his tee shot and asked, "Where did that go?" Scorpy peered blankly ahead and finally slurred, "Where did what go?"

Interestingly, the course does not appear to be any easier in dry conditions. The 1977 PGA Championship was held during a drought that was so severe that large cracks appeared in the earth. It may have been the only time in a major championship that players were given permission to lift from the cracked earth without penalty. Bill Spence, who has since moved on to become the green superintendent at The Country Club in Brookline, Massachusetts, was the superintendent at Pebble Beach then. "The drought was so bad we had to go to court to get permission to water the greens," Spence recalls. "What fascinated me, though, was the fact that the design of Pebble Beach emerged in a way the players had not experienced before. The ball would bounce into fairway con-

tours in unfamiliar areas, which brought into play many hazards and subtleties of the course that previously had been ignored." The tournament was won by Lanny Wadkins with 282, the same score that Watson posted when he took the U.S. Open title five years later. The difficulty of Pebble Beach has not been overstated. In the 1972 U.S. Open, which Nicklaus won, it was almost embarrassing to observe that one-third of the field of 150 players, the best in the game, could not break 80 in either the first or the second rounds. Byron Nelson has played the game about as well as anyone has, particularly the long game, and a course like Pebble Beach with its demand for long striking, would seem to be tailored to his game. "I never found Pebble Beach easy," Nelson says. "It may start off easy, but you'd better have your score on the card before you get to number seven, because you won't make up much ground after that. I think the sequence from seven through ten is one of the most challenging stretches of golf I've ever seen. And those two holes at the end of the course are so difficult that sometimes, on the holes leading up to them, you feel pressure to take chances that you shouldn't."

In 1988, Pebble Beach hosted

the $2 million Nabisco Championship, the richest event in golf. The winner was Curtis Strange. Pebble Beach has held nine national championships. The last one in 1992, when Tom Kite, in extremely heavy wind, sealed his victory on the short par three seventh. His tee shot wound up in the rear bunker. He had a down hill, down grain shot with hardly any green. He was looking at bogey or worse. But as fate would have it, his shot hit the flagstick and dropped. It was going fast enough to have made it half way to Salinas. He did not look back.

Whether it is played in bad weather or good, for a national championship or just a casual round, Pebble Beach will probably remain what it has always been, an authentic and accessible treasure. Because it is open to the public, it is one of a handful of the world's great golf courses that can be played by anyone with the price of admission and the willingness to endure its majestic hardships. And if you are able to play it well, it is a course that will reward you as much as any you will ever play.

The hour-glass seventeenth green has made
the difference to many a competition.
Remember Tom Watson's chip-in?

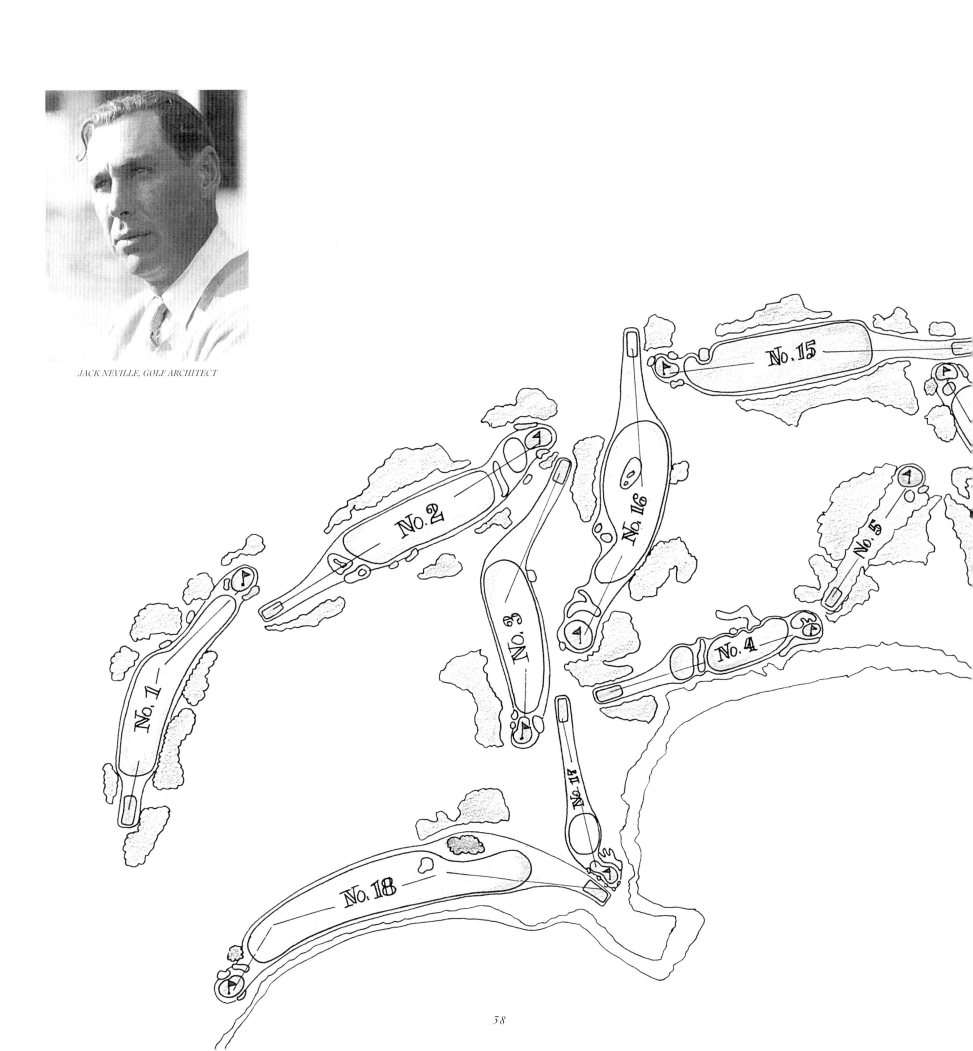

JACK NEVILLE, GOLF ARCHITECT

No. 15

No. 2

No. 16

No. 5

No. 3

No. 1

No. 4

No. 17

No. 18

PEBBLE BEACH GOLF LINKS

COURSE RATING: 75.0

HOLE	1	2	3	4	5	6	7	8	9		10	11	12	13	14	15	16	17	18		
PAR	4	5	4	4	3	5	3	4	4	36	4	4	3	4	5	4	4	3	5	36	72
YARDS	373	502	388	327	166	516	107	431	464	3,274	426	384	202	392	565	397	402	209	548	3,525	6,799

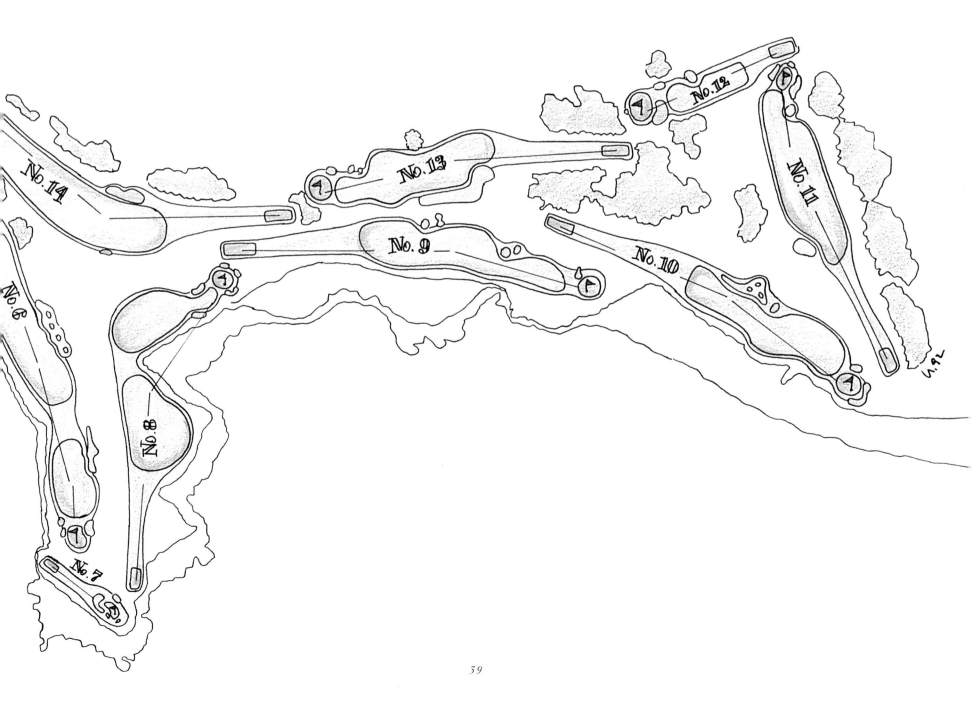

Spyglass Hill Golf Course

*T*HE PLEASURES OF GOLF, SUCH as they are, are never more tantalizing than when we see them in our imaginations as we anticipate the game ahead. Among the pleasures of golf on the Monterey Peninsula, I count its peaceful roadways that afford such an agreeable means of getting from place to place. These roadways are simple affairs, nothing more than country lanes that wind through the Del Monte Forest. There are no sidewalks, no gutters, no street lights, just rustic passages among the trees that travel past half-hidden fairways and the elegant, secluded homes that rest upon the wooded hillsides. As one travels along, there is time to absorb the feel and smell of the place, to settle one's mind and body into the rhythms of the surroundings and to contemplate the day's adventures. If you follow one of these lanes out past the polo field and equestrian center you will come to the Spyglass Hill Golf Course, just beyond Cypress Point around a bend in the road. The clubhouse, small and unobtrusive, nestles quietly among scattered pines. There is little to suggest that this is the most powerful and feared golf course on the peninsula, indeed one of the most powerful in America.

Spyglass Hill is feared only in the sense that it is so remorseless in exposing golfing weaknesses, for otherwise it is a course of immense beauty and visual surprises. It opens in the dunesland, with views of the ocean, before plunging deep into the forest past grazing deer and tall Monterey pines that line the fairways like sentinels.

The creator of Spyglass Hill is Robert Trent Jones, who has said that the contrast between these settings inspired him to model the holes after Pine Valley, in the dunes, and Augusta National, in the forest. When the course opened in 1966, Jones was at the height of his powers, the most

widely recognized golf architect of his time, perhaps of any time. Jones has designed more than four hundred golf courses all over the world, and probably has exerted a greater influence on the game than any man of his lifetime. In the 1940s and 1950s, he had revolutionized golf course design and forged it into an industry. Long before Palmer and Nicklaus began to set up networks of designers, artists, builders, construction and maintenance crews, financiers and the like, Jones had done so. His empire reached around the world and his modern golf courses played a significant role in fomenting a global interest in the game, particularly in countries like Spain and those in the Caribbean basin. Many of his courses have stirred controversy, and certainly Spyglass Hill has, but even his rivals agree that Jones is the most successful golf architect of them all. And in his eighties, Jones is still going strong. Living half his life on airplanes, the other half divided more or less equally between meetings with the movers and shakers who have become his clients, and sessions at the drawing board with his staff. Sleep is for mortals.

Robert Trent Jones is an amiable and cultured man who has studied the game in depth and has written about it with great skill and understanding. He is a self-made man who set out deliberately to become what he has become, in an era when hard knocks were easier to come by than hard cash. Jones was aided by his engaging personality, a tough core that gave a resonance to his strong views about golf design. It was, and still is, a very appealing and democratic message: that every player should have a fair chance, but those who aspire to the highest rewards would, as so often happens in life, face the harshest penalties. Jones believes that a golf hole should be a hard par and easy bogey, a philosophy that is expressed forthrightly at Spyglass Hill.

This sanctity of par became a Jones trademark while there was almost always a safe alternative that would produce a bogey there was not much room for mistakes if one looked to do better. One gets the feeling in playing his courses that, to make a par, one is expected to hit good shots all the time, and to make birdie the shots should be pretty close to wonderful. This is exactly what Jones wants, and he wants it to be felt most by the professional players.

This is a point of view that is not shared by many of the professionals, especially when the course has been designed by Jones. Ever

The fifteenth, page 40, tumbles through the forest to a boomerang-shaped green, one of two par threes on the back nine that play from the same hill, but in different directions.

The third hole, at right, is a par three that plays from atop a dune toward the ocean—a tempting prize with the foreboding name "th Black Spot."

since Jones redesigned the Oakland Hills course for the 1951 United States Open, a course that Ben Hogan called a "monster" even though he won the tournament, the professionals have been leery of Jones and have tended to approach his newer courses with as much affection as they would a coiled viper.

After playing Spyglass Hill for the first time in the 1967 Bing Crosby Tournament, the pros offered these strained, if colorful, reactions: "This course is built right around my game," said George Archer. "It touches no part of it." Bob Rosburg said that it was the toughest course he had ever played, from green to tee. A colleague who preferred anonymity said that he had played the course "under unfortunate conditions; it was open." One of the shorter-hitting professionals said that he had trouble playing par fours that were designed for King Kong.

Another, a combat veteran, said that he preferred it to hand-to-hand combat. The more they complained, the more broadly Jones smiled. After watching the pros stagger from the course, day after day, mumbling amongst themselves about the greens they were four-putting, about the 80s they couldn't break, about the 90s some of them were looking at for the first time in

The long sinuous green at the fourth hole is a fascinating example of the links style, tucked away betwen the dunes on this shortish par four.

their professional lives, sportswriter Jim Murray had seen enough. There was something about these performances that warmed Murray's heart, an organ that customarily is not without its icy tinges.

"If it were human," Murray wrote, "Spyglass Hill would have a knife in its teeth, a patch on its eye, a ring in its ear, tobacco in its beard. It is a privateer plundering the golfing main, an amphibious creature, half ocean, half forest. It's a 200-acre unplayable lie." Thereafter, the pros were inclined to hold a very high opinion of Mr. Murray. Later on, it was generally agreed that the course was not ready for that first tournament, that the greens were too new and thin, that the brush had not yet been cleared from the forest and rough, that flagsticks had been placed in awkward spots, and that it was nearly impossible at its full length of 7,200 yards.

These problems have long since disappeared and Spyglass Hill, now shortened to 6,810 yards, has fully matured. Its fairways and greens have ripened into lush, beautifully conditioned ribbons of turf that flash between the trees. Even so, it remains an excruciating test of golf. For more than twenty years, it has consistently produced the highest scores of the three Crosby Tournament courses. "I always felt that if you could get out of there with even par, you were stealing something," Bob Rosburg says. "The year I won the Crosby, I shot 72, at Spyglass, and I think that's the lowest score I've ever had there."

The first hole sweeps downhill, a long par five that curves majestically to the left and carries you out of the forest and onto the dunesland. It is a wonderful opening hole with plenty of space, at 600 yards, to stretch and loosen the muscles. The next four holes are laid among the dunes in a sequence that is well supplied with charm and interest. The second hole is a slender little baggage, the fairway darting between the dunes and tall sea grasses to a smallish green that is appropriate to its length. The third hole is a one-shotter, played from atop a dune to the green far below, with a panoramic view that takes in the bathers at Fanshell Beach and the sea lions basking on Seal Rock. The fourth is a fascinating par four that curls gently to the left between two dunes to a long, sinuous green, a splendid example of the links style. The course is beginning to stretch out here; the next hole, an uphill par three of 180 yards, asks for a crisp stroke with a longish iron. By this time the juices should be flowing, and you will need them because the course then climbs into the forest.

Three of the next four holes are long, uphill par fours that are interrupted briefly by the par five seventh, which plays downhill. The eighth not only goes uphill, it does so by means of a very narrow fairway with a severe dropoff to the right, and the ninth is quite long. By this time, you are beginning to get an idea of what the rest of the course will be like.

One of the things that makes Spyglass Hill so difficult is that its greens are crowned, like a saucer turned upside down, and many of them are elevated above the fairway. Approach shots that land on the aprons or the edges of these greens are liable to kick into a bunker, or at the very least trickle away from the hole. And unless you can place the approach shot in the vicinity of the hole, putting over the rolling greens can be a tiresome business. Another feature, less obvious but nevertheless persistent, is that so many of the greenside bunkers are shaped, with almost diabolical cunning, so that the sandy slopes tend to rise toward the outside of the hole. The effect of this is that, often enough to be vexing, bunker shots are

The sixteenth is a murderous hole, at 465 yards
it is the longest par four
at Spyglass Hill.

played from a downhill lie toward unreceptive greens. In fairness, it should be noted that one must hit the ball rather far off line to reach these spots. Jones is such an agreeable fellow, though. Is is possible that he does not trust me to hit my shots reasonably straight?

Finally, if you do not drive the ball well at Spyglass Hill, you will experience a day of tribulation. I can think of few inland courses, perhaps Olympic and Medinah, where bad driving is treated so harshly. Length alone, though sorely needed, is not enough because trees, gulleys and ravines hug almost every hole. There are places, easily reached from the tee, that not even a grizzly bear would visit. As the holes roll by, you begin to sense a pressure that gradually builds and becomes relentless. This pressure is most intense at the par fours, which seem to play so much longer than the yardages shown on the scorecard. The reasons for this lie in the structure of the greens and the greenside bunkers and the fact that most of the par fours are played uphill and to elevated greens. There is really no letup. Each hole is strong and suits its own purpose. Most golf courses, even great golf courses, have holes that are dull or weak, or are somehow flawed. Spyglass Hill

has no obvious flaws. It comes at you in a sequence that is balanced and sound, one strong hole after another. Even the finishing holes, which are not as climactic nor as decisive as one might want, are splendid individual holes.

The second nine begins on the crest of a hill, and it is something of a relief to discover that the next few holes are played downhill. The tenth swings around to the left and there, just at the turn of the dogleg in the center of the fairway, Jones has left some trees, as if to remind us of the chief hazard that encloses us on all sides. This side travels through severe terrain, with sudden shifts in elevation which Jones has dealt with by creating two par threes that play from the same hill, in different directions. The 180-yard twelfth falls steeply downhill with a pond on the left, and the 130-yard fifteenth descends less severely to a boomerang-shaped green with a pond on the right.

The sixteenth, the longest par four on the course at 465 yards is a murderous hole that plays from a high tee across a ravine to a fairway that bends to the right and has ravines on both sides. Interestingly, this monster is shaped so that the most advantageous way to attack the hole from the tee is to produce a power fade, one of the more diffi-

cult shots to summon when the pressure is on. The designer has shaped the hole in such a way that an aggressive player is almost forced to hit a particular shot if he wants to obtain maximum advantage of the hole. The fairway falls to a small green with wicked bunkering on the left, so an approach from that side will be not only longer but infinitely less appealing. It didn't seem to bother Sam Snead, though, when he played the course for the first time during the 1968 Bing Crosby Tournament. Even Jones, the resolute defender of par, had to smile at the way Snead played the hole. He hit a drive, a six-iron and a putt. Birdie. Never said a word, just strolled through the trees whistling on his way to the next hole. That's one way, or you try to play safe and make an easy six. Jones is proud of the fact that his creation, in spite of Snead, has withstood the onslaughts of succeeding generations of golfers. When he was asked to design the course, in a neighborhood that already had two of the world's most famous courses, Jones admits that his own competitive instincts were stirred. "I wanted to make it the best and toughest test of golf on the Monterey Peninsula, and I think we succeeded," Jones said

The serene setting of the twelfth, a par three
of about 180 downhill yards,
can easily put unrealistic thoughts into the golfers mind.

recently, "although it's not as tough as it once was. The ball is different today, and so the shot values have changed." It is a relief to hear it, although what that means to most of us as we get on in the game is that we will be needing at least one more club.

Fundamental to Jones' philosophy is his belief that shorter hitters should be given a fair chance without granting them an undue advantage, so the difference between playing the white and blue tees is one of degree. From the shorter tees, Spyglass Hill retains much of its character and strength, but will not murder the longer-handicap player. This flexibility was important in the concept because Spyglass Hill was organized by the Northern California Golf Association to be its headquarters course. Bob Hanna headed the organization in those days. "We needed a place to stage our own tournaments, " Hanna says. "What place could you choose that is better than the Monterey Peninsula? Sam Morse agreed to help, and we worked out a lease arrangement to share the course with Pebble Beach Company. So it was important that the course be designed in such a way that the public could play it, too. The only instructions we gave Jones were to

stay out of an old Indian village between the present sixth and seventh holes, and to build the greatest test of golf that he could. Did he succeed? You bet he did. If you want to find out how well you can play the game, go play Spyglass Hill." With the opening of Poppy Hills and the move of the Northern California Golf Association to the new facility, Spyglass Hill is now owned and operated by Pebble Beach Company as a public course. Spyglass Hill is named in honor of Robert Louis Stevenson, who lived for a time in a house overlooking the beach, where he wrote many of his stories. Stevenson, who seems to have been one of the few Scots whose passions were not governed by golf and whiskey, had been so taken with the Monterey Peninsula that he described it as "the most beautiful meeting of land and water that nature has produced." It is said that the setting inspired Stevenson to write his classic tale, *Treasure Island*, a notion that appealed to Sam Morse. The holes are named for characters and landmarks in Stevenson's book—Black Dog, Long John Silver, Blind Pew, Skeleton Cove, the Black Spot and Billy Bones. Such are the cheerful and appropriate images that accompany one's adventures at Spyglass Hill. For all of its menace,

The tenth hole plays downhill around a bend in the forest. In the center of the fairway is a line of trees, as if to remind players of the chief hazard that surrounds them on all sides.

The eleventh hole, pages 54—55, swings downhill with an approach across a pond that sprawls in front of the green.

and perhaps because of it, Spyglass Hill is enormously popular. Part of the fun, I think, is the knowledge of how much sorrow it inflicts on the top professionals. Part of it comes from a sense of seclusion and stunning contrasts in the landscape that arouse our interest and admiration. Not long ago, a visiting British golfing society spent a week playing the Monterey Peninsula courses and proclaimed a strong preference for Spyglass Hill over its more famous neighbor, Pebble Beach, for both the quality of its play and its beauty. This seems to be a fairly representative attitude among the general golfing public, which keeps the course filled even on days when the weather is miserable.

In playing a course like Spyglass Hill, you will be reminded soon enough that golf is more than a game of striking the ball well. It is a trial of the inner man, and if Spyglass Hill is anything it is a course that asks for powers of concentration, patience and composure. Dr. Samuel Johnson once observed that the contemplation of one's own execution concentrates the mind wonderfully. Somehow, this notion seems to fit Spyglass Hill rather well. Isn't it curious that it would pop into my thoughts just now?

One of the few straight-forward holes on the course, the long par four thirteenth provides a brief respite from the tactical decisions that precede it—and those that are to come.

SPYGLASS HILL GOLF COURSE

COURSE RATING: 76.1

HOLE	1	2	3	4	5	6	7	8	9		10	11	12	13	14	15	16	17	18		
PAR	5	4	3	4	3	4	5	4	4	36	4	5	3	4	5	3	4	4	4	36	72
YARDS	600	350	150	365	180	415	515	395	425	3,395	400	520	180	440	555	130	465	320	405	3,415	6,810

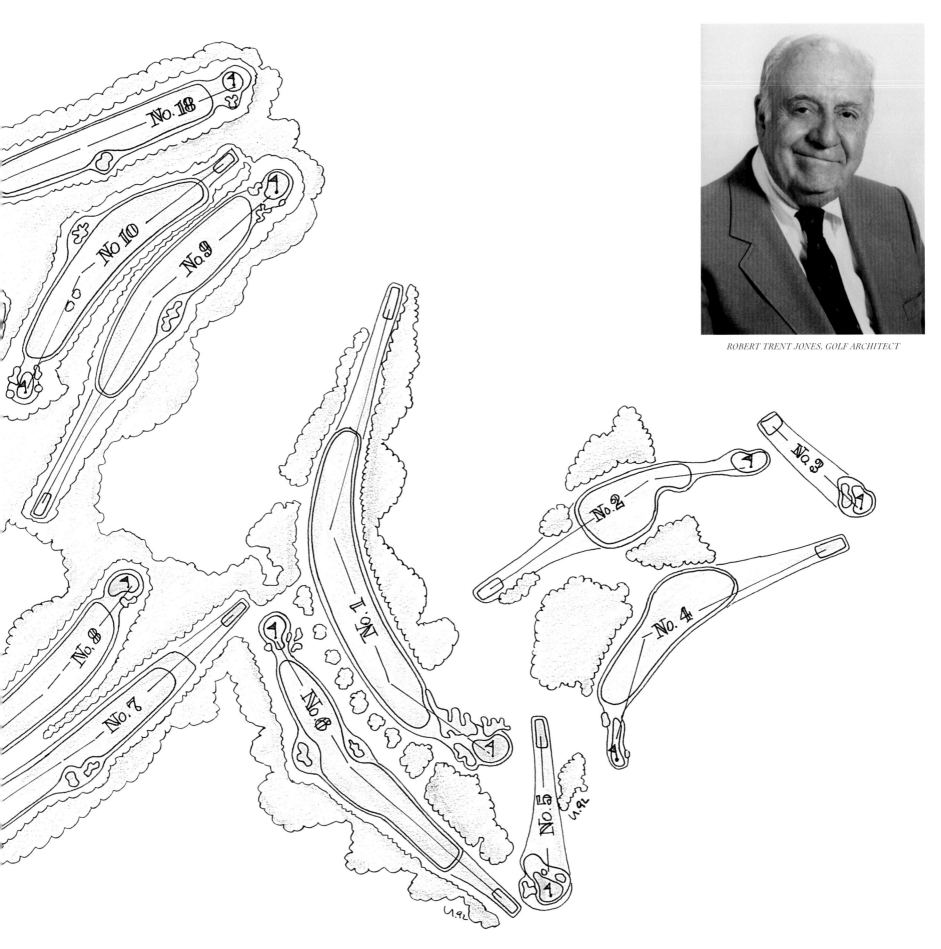

ROBERT TRENT JONES, GOLF ARCHITECT

Cypress Point Club

IF THE OBJECT OF JUSTICE IS TO be fair and impartial, to make the punishment fit the crime, then none of us would be allowed to play Cypress Point. For all of us are sinners and Cypress Point is the kind of place that inspires golfers to have downright religious thoughts. Some have been so moved that they refer to it as the Sistine Chapel of Golf, an extravagance that is probably forgivable in a place that invites the extravagant phrase.

There is another line associated with Cypress Point that is heard often enough that it approaches an article of faith: "If I were condemned to play only one course for the rest of my life, I would choose Cypress Point." No one is certain who was the first to offer this opinion but it is shared by a surprising number of well-known players and authorities in the game, including Joseph C. Dey, Tom Watson, Ken Venturi, Deane Beman, Sandy Tatum, Bob

Rosburg, Dave Marr and Harvie Ward. There are reasons, of course, for these high opinions, but people have used too many superlatives to describe Cypress Point that we tend to forget it is a golf course.

It occupies the edge of a headland, from which the course gets its name, that juts into the Pacific Ocean and folds inland across rolling forest and dunesland. The clubhouse is a simple white structure that occupies the highest elevation of the property. It was designed in the Monterey Colonial style by a prominent California architect named George Washington Smith, who sited the building so ingeniously among the native cypress trees that it seems almost to have grown from the spot. A public road cuts through the property, an unexpected hazard that must be carried from the first tee. The opening hole starts a few paces from the plain wooden golf shop that also houses the locker room, sweeping inland

down the hill and then up another, a par four that curves gently to the right. Because of its length, 421 yards, and the uphill second shot to a plateau green, it is a shade more difficult than the ideal opening hole.

Oddly enough, this widely admired golf course contains a number of design curiosities. For one thing, it can hardly be described as well balanced, in the conventional sense, even though leading golf magazines have asserted otherwise. It is the only course of national reputation and standing that contains back-to-back par fives, in the middle of the front nine, and consecutive par threes, near the end. Another curiosity is consecutive par fours in the dunes at the end of the front nine, both very short and very similar in concept but quite different in shape and feel. Finally, Cypress Point has a strangely cramped and ungainly finishing hole, a shortish par four that doglegs awkwardly uphill past a bewildering picket of cypress trees that give an illusion of occupying the entire fairway. The hole measures just 346 yards and, for the good player, would normally require little more than two solid iron shots, but it can be a ghastly experience when the wind is up and the last thing you can afford is an indifferent shot. It is a hole that

you sometimes feel you grope toward, rather than play. Yet the architect must have sensed that this doesn't much matter, for it comes after three smashing, incomparable holes along the ocean, perhaps he felt that the soft dissolve at the eighteenth with the green perched just below the clubhouse would be an acceptable, even fitting contrast to what had come before.

There are good reasons for pointing out these curious features, for despite the absence of a more conventional design balance, Cypress Point flows with an almost majestic beauty from one hole setting to the next. It unfolds with a sublime inevitability that few have had reason to question. It might have been otherwise. The man originally chosen to design the course was Seth Raynor, a construction man who had worked for Charles Blair MacDonald on The National Golf Links on Long Island, New York, and then had designed a new course for the Chicago Golf Club, which MacDonald had started. Raynor had been brought to the Monterey Peninsula to design the Monterey Peninsula course for Sam Morse, who died before completing the job and before the Cypress Point job began. The organizers, headed by Roger Lapham and Marion Hollins,

The first hole, above curls downhill around a clump of cypress that catches many tee shots, then climbs uphill to a slick plateau green. The course moves inland at the long second where the stern phalanx of bunkers, as shown in the photo at right, guards access to the wide fairway shelf on the preferred but most dangerous line of attack.

On the opening page, a grizzled cypress tree, ravaged by the elements, stubbornly guards the approach to the sixteenth green.

a former U.S. Women's Open champion who worked for Morse, then turned to Dr. Alister MacKenzie. MacKenzie had just completed The Valley Club, a lovely course in Santa Barbara whose merits have gone largely unappreciated. MacKenzie was a Scot, and a medical man who well understood the relationship of man to the environment and the healthful effects of golf on the human mind and body. He was also a man who well understood the game of golf, perhaps as well as any man who has chosen to practice the art of golf design, although he was not a particularly good player. His works, which later were to include the Augusta National course in Georgia and Royal Melbourne in Australia, reveal a man whose obvious feel for the game was guided by a fine grasp of proportion and an uncanny sense for the artistic line.

How his heart must have warmed as he explored the site, for here he found an astonishing range of golfing and vegetational settings —parkland, forest, desert dunes and oceanside. In the hands of a lesser man this might have seemed interesting, but not essential. One of the marvels of Cypress Point is how smoothly MacKenzie made the transitions between these different settings, how effortlessly the

holes blend with the terrain and how naturally they fit into the landscape. Each of the holes occupies a space and a scale to match its setting, and at the same time they are in scale with one another. So while there is a certain imbalance in the design, there is a harmony between the holes themselves and the natural world through which they move. It is this sense of harmony, I think, that makes Cypress Point so compel-ling and so richly satisfying to play.

Fast greens are another compelling and sometimes maddening characteristic of Cypress Point. The turf is mostly Poa annua, including the greens, but is carefully managed and groomed. The putting surfaces are polished to the consistency of porcelain. Hank Ketcham, who has been playing Cypress Point for forty years and has been a member since 1977 explains: "Under normal conditions, you can't attack the hole because the greens are so slippery. On some holes, it's like putting in a bathtub and trying to stop the ball short of the drain. You'll notice this especially on the greens that are pitched into the hillsides, like the first, the fourth and eighteenth."

The course moves inland from the opening hole, into the forest where the holes are models of sylvan

beauty and solitude. After the consecutive par fives at the fifth and sixth, the short seventh hole leads into a large hilly dune, a splendid par three that provides a transition into the finish of the front nine.

Here MacKenzie created two short par fours that are as demanding and, especially in the wind, as exciting and troublesome as any in golf. The fairways are mere flecks of green against the huge, unkempt wildness of the dunes. One is tempted to use the driver, as one always is on a short par four, but the fairways are so narrow that no sensible fellow would risk a hopeless lie in the unruly wasteland. One decides to use an iron club, but if there is wind will the second shot be tougher than the first? And so the battle rages inside oneself; it is a classic example of the course designer's forcing the player to choose between two unappealing alternatives. Unless one has the talent and composure to hit the ball straight and reasonably long, one gets the impression that a bow and arrow might work better. Both holes are cunningly conceived, and yet are tempting birdie chances for the brave and untroubled mind. MacKenzie must have possessed a wonderful imagination to have seen these two holes in that dune. Sandy Tatum has been a member of

The sixth hole, the second
of the consecutive par five
inland holes, sweeps
majestically downhill to a green
that is perched into the side
of a dune, a setting of
magnificent solitude.

Cypress Point for many years and still shakes his head when he talks about these holes.

"If you can conceive of what that dune must have looked like in its native state, you have to conclude that MacKenzie was touched by more than imagination. It took real genius to have created two such wonderful holes. He has created what amounts to about six hundred yards of par eight, each hole approximately three hundred yards and each an absolutely fascinating golf hole. Collectively, back to back, I think they are just about the most interesting shortish par fours that there are in the world," Tatum says.

From the dune, the second nine heads back into a parkland setting, with two long holes, then heads out to the sea with two holes that fetch up against the dunes and another that sweeps up to a gentle crest of the headland. Beyond is the crashing climax of the course, consecutive par threes at the fifteenth and sixteenth and a majestic par four at the seventeenth. Who in golf has not seen the sixteenth, either in person or in photographs, or perhaps in a dream? It is probably the most famous single hole in golf, and more often than not it is the one players talk about after the round is over. It is the kind of

The awesome and hauntingly beutiful sixteenth, shown on pages 66–67, is probably the most famous hole in golf.
It occupies the very tip of Cypress Point, surrounded by jagged rocks and swirling eddies of the sea.
Above, the seventeenth, from behind the green looking back to the tee.

hole that players think about even before the round begins. Tom Watson is not alone in saying, "Every time I play Cypress Point I think about the sixteenth, what the conditions will be and how I'll play it." Dave Marr, taking a view somewhere between H.L. Mencken and Edgar Allan Poe, says: "All day you're twisting in the wind, waiting for the sixteenth to appear."

The dictionary defines the word awesome as "inspiring a feeling of wonder, fear, reverence, terror and dread caused by something majestic, sublime or possessing the quality of grandeur." That's a reasonable description of the sixteenth, where the golfer must play across the heaving ocean and jagged rocks to a promontory upon which sits the green, some 233 yards away. To the right, nothing but ocean; to the left, there is a bailout area on the peninsula that leads to the green, a route that is preordained on those occasions when the wind is in your teeth. The green is elevated above the ocean some twenty to thirty feet and is surrounded by thick, fleshy ice plant, which is one of nature's most revolting hazards. Even the best players dread having to escape from this mushy growth. One imagines they would prefer boiling oil. One unhappy gentleman, a respected touring pro of his

day named Hans Merrill, drove onto the tiny beach below the green and had the misfortune of taking nineteen strokes going from rock to rock, ice plant to ice plant, before holing out in a display of stubborn exhaustion. Ed "Porky" Oliver once recorded a sixteen there in a fifty miles per hour gale, after hitting six provisional balls into the ocean. He made the green in fourteen and got down in two. On the other hand, Bing Crosby once made a hole in one at the sixteenth, a feat that has been accomplished, surprisingly, seven times. The great thing about the sixteenth is that it is a challenge that few egomaniacs can resist, regardless of the level of their skill. And which of us can suppress those manly instincts when such an obvious and threatening target is in view? It is such a daunting and challenging hole that some have claimed MacKenzie originally conceived of it as a short par four, but all the reliable evidence suggests otherwise, and if we can be sure of one thing it is that MacKenzie knew a great one-shot hole when he saw one.

As dramatic and beautiful as the sixteenth is, there are many who believe that the preceding hole has greater merit as a par three. The fifteenth is the first of three ocean holes, and is blessed with

one of the loveliest settings in golf. It is relatively short, at 143 yards, and plays from an elevated tee across a rocky chasm into a triangular green that is attractively accented by sand bunkers. Providing a back-drop is a thick stand of cypress, with the ocean boiling in from the right. A simple dirt path leads along the edge of the cliff from the tee to the green, and one of the delights of this hole is to walk along and watch the mother seals teaching their young to swim in the narrow inlet below. Near the green are patches of grassy rough, and ice plant, with unpredictable swirling winds. The green sits like a glimmering emerald amidst all this, inviting a bold and determined stroke. It is a hole of eminently fair proportions, a test of skill and judgment, a visual feast, and taken altogether is one of the jewels of golf.

The final member of this oceanside triumvirate of holes, the seventeenth, is a breathtaking panorama that plays back across a corner of the ocean with a forced carry followed by a spine-tingling second shot. As you gaze from the tee you can see the fairway angling to the right and running along the edge of the rocky headland and, in the distance, the flagstick outlined against the bay some 393 yards away. After a long carry, as heroic

A striking example of the genius of Alister MacKenzie is the creation of the eighth and ninth, the short par fours in the dunes. This view shows the ninth green in the foregroud, with the eighth hole rising to its sentinel green at the right.

as you dare, the approach must be played around or over a monstrous clump of cypress that sprawls in the middle of the fairway to a green that clings precariously close to the cliff and is not all that large. Under normal conditions it is a genuine, full-blooded two-shotter, and when the wind whips in from the ocean it is no place for the timid. During the Crosby Tournament one year, with the wind howling, Jimmy Demaret played the seventeenth with two drivers: "I aimed both of 'em out over the ocean, and they blew back." he grinned. "And I was short at that; had to chip up for my par."

When the round is over, players repair to the simple surroundings of the locker room to swap stories or to lick their wounds. What is most pleasing is that everything at Cypress Point, except for the golf course, is understated. The clubhouse has one large room, a lounge, a small dining room and an enclosed porch that overlooks the holes along the ocean toward the west. Upstairs are four sleeping rooms for out-of-town members or guests. It is evident that the members have felt no urge to compete with the furnishings of nature. The membership level has been kept at around 240, most of whom live elsewhere, and efforts to

increase it are gently and firmly resisted. Bob Hope, a former member, once joked about this, saying: "When Cypress Point had a membership drive, they drove out forty members." Fiction, of course, but what this illustrates is that Cypress Point attracts people of accomplishment and means who dearly love their golf, and who care enough to preserve some of its more enjoyable values. Over the years, Cypress Point has acquired the patina of age and tradition that one associates with a valued masterpiece. But unlike a painting, the tradition is renewed every day, every time there is another game. Cypress Point has been the scene of some memorable games, including one of the greatest matches of this century. It was a match that almost nobody saw and yet one that continues to be talked about by those who follow the game closely. It was a classic four-ball confrontation between two of the game's greatest professionals, Ben Hogan and Byron Nelson, and the two greatest amateurs of the day, E. Harvie Ward and Ken Venturi. The match took place in January 1956, just before the Bing Crosby Tournament and, like many happy accidents, was hatched at a cocktail party before one of the practice rounds. Hogan was then at the

The twelfth green, in the photo at right, fetches up against a windswept dune overlooking the crashing surf.

The eighteenth hole, in the photo above, is approached through a bewildering picket of cypress trees that sometimes give an illusion of occupying the entire fairway.

height of his powers, a man who many believed was the best player in the history of golf. There was nothing that he could not do with a golf ball. Nelson had retired from active competition, but whenever he emerged from his ranch in Roanoke, Texas, he was a dangerous man who seemed to have lost none of his awesome skill. Hogan was a great driver, but Nelson was a better one, and his peers say that no one before or since could hit long irons like Lord Byron. Harvie Ward was the reigning United States Amateur champion. He had won the British Amateur title in 1952, and would win the U.S. title again in 1956. He played with a relaxed composure born of a simple swing and a sound method that was finished off with a wonderful putting touch and a flair for the winning stroke. Ken Venturi had just beaten Ward in the San Francisco City Championship at Harding Park. Ward had been four under par for thirty-two holes and still Venturi had won, three and two, and with no other worlds to conquer he was about to turn professional. There are those who swear that, even then, Venturi could hit golf shots that would make the angels blush.

Few people who sit around at cocktail parties dreaming up fantasy

The short fifteenth hole is a glimmering jewel that plays across a rocky chasm to a lovely green setting surrounded by bunkers and backed by a thicket of cypress.

golf matches can actually pull it off, but George Coleman and Eddie Lowery could. Coleman, a wealthy businessman and well-traveled golfer, was the host of the party. He was a member of many fine clubs, including Seminole, of which he is currently the president. Lowery who had caddied for Francis Ouimet when he won the U.S. Amateur in 1913, had become a successful automobile dealer, which enabled him to indulge his lifelong passion which was golf. He was an active USGA man and took a special interest in helping out promising amateurs, among them Venturi and Ward. Lowery felt they could beat anybody, and said so at the party, and after some more conversation a bet was arrived at with Lowery backing his amateurs against whomever Coleman wanted to pick. He chose Hogan and Nelson.

Only a handful of people showed up the next day to see the match because Hogan did not want a large gallery, and a fake tee time had been arranged at Pebble Beach. As the match began, the players must have sensed that this was one of those occasions, rare even then but unheard of today, when money was the last thing on anyone's mind. When Nelson was asked, thirty-two years later, to recall the match, he said: "It was

the best four-ball match I ever played, in fact it was the best one I ever saw. Those kids didn't back off from anybody. They could play, and they came ready to play."

It became apparent, as the match wore on, that none of these players would back off. Between the four men there were twenty-seven birdies and an eagle. Neither side could gain the advantage and the issue remained in doubt until the final putt of the final hole. On the par five tenth hole, Hogan spun an eighty-five yard wedge shot into the hole for an eagle to put the professionals one up. On the eleventh, a long and difficult par four, Nelson whistled a two-iron to within twenty feet of the flagstick and sank the putt, but Venturi matched his birdie, and the players halved every hole thereafter. At the short fifteenth, Hogan and Venturi both made birdies. On the sixteenth, where both men hit drivers, Ward and Nelson each made a two. On the seventeenth, the par four along the cliff, Ward and Nelson again made birdies. At the eighteenth, the match came down to birdie putts by Venturi and Hogan. Venturi holed his from twelve feet, and then watched Hogan line up his ten-footer. Just before he putted, Hogan was heard to mutter, "I'm not about to be tied

The serene parkland setting of the eleventh hole belies its stern character. This 437-yard hole is rated the most difficult par four on the Monterey Peninsula, and was the second toughest on the professional tour when Cypress Point Club was part of the Crosby Clambake.

by two so-and-so amateurs." With characteristic steely purpose he ran the putt into the hole on top of Venturi, and the professionals had won. Barely. "I hate to lose," Venturi says, "but I just had to love it when Ben drained it at eighteen. We played our best and, at least on that day, we got beat by the best. Isn't that what makes golf a great game?" The match had produced a wonderful burst of scoring: Ward and Nelson each shot 67, Venturi scored 65 and Hogan 63. It is interesting that a golf course with so much beauty and scenery could somehow bring out the best in such players. Years later, Nelson offered this explanation: "Cypress Point is one of the most inspiring places in the world to play this game, and it is the kind of course where, if you play really well, you can score." And this, it seems to me, is what golfers dream about, a course that will treat mistakes harshly, but one where the reward for patience, skill, composure and daring are so plainly attainable. It is this quality that MacKenzie surely had in mind when he laid out the course, a quality that elevates Cypress Point from the ranks of just another pretty face into greatness, a place where the most satisfying test of golf, those of the mind and the imagination, are so richly and agreeably fulfilled.

The spectacular seventeenth, shown on pages 78–79, runs along the rocky headland, skirting the rugged cliffs, a scene that inspires equal measures of dread and admiration. The approach to the green must be played over, or around, the fat cypress tree in the middle of the fairway.

Another view of the seventeenth shows this from a different angle in the aerial photograph to the right.

CYPRESS POINT CLUB

COURSE RATING: 72.3

HOLE	1	2	3	4	5	6	7	8	9		10	11	12	13	14	15	16	17	18		
PAR	4	5	3	4	4	5	3	4	4	37	5	4	4	4	4	3	3	4	4	35	72
YARDS	421	548	162	384	493	518	168	363	292	3,349	480	437	404	365	388	143	231	393	346	3,187	6,536

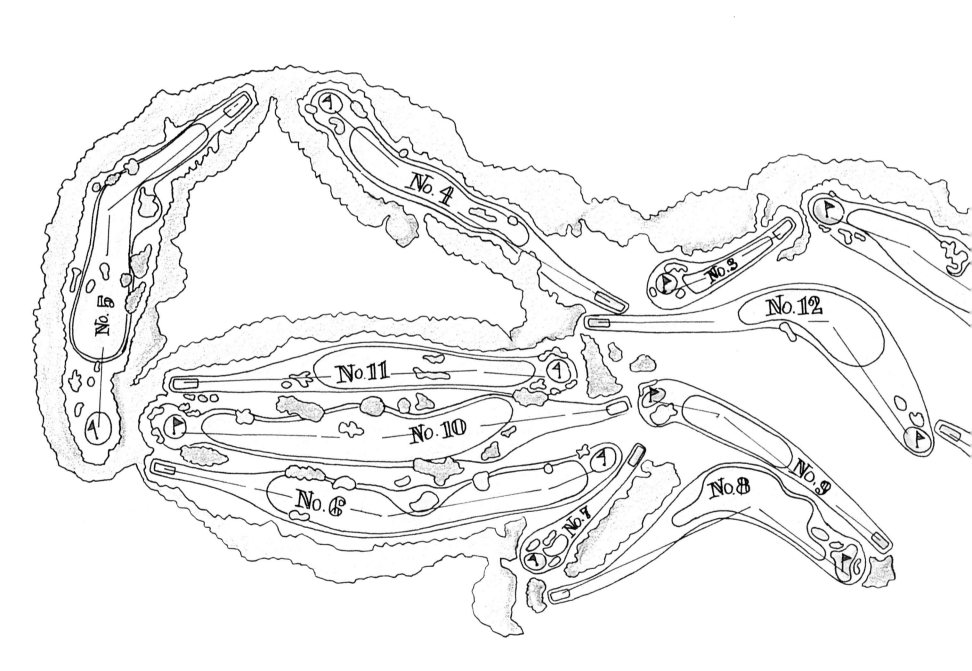

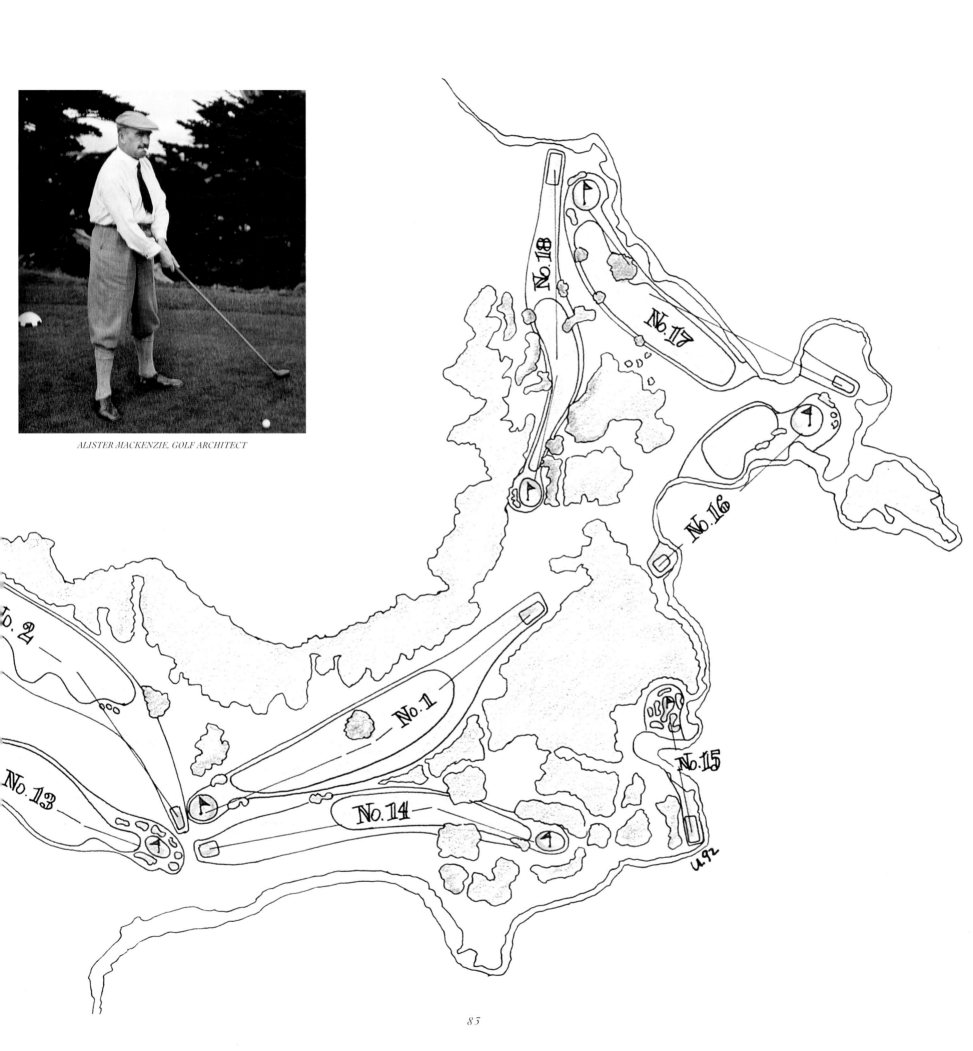

ALISTER MACKENZIE, GOLF ARCHITECT

No. 18

No. 17

No. 16

No. 2

No. 1

No. 13

No. 14

No. 15

Poppy Hills Golf Course

*F*EW PLACES ON EARTH CAN match the Monterey Peninsula in the diversity of its golfing landscape. From the shoreline to the interior of the Del Monte Forest is but a short distance, scarcely more than a brisk walk, but the settings are worlds apart. As one moves inland, the terrain piles up into rugged hills and ravines, rising in places to nearly one thousand feet above the nearby ocean. There, tumbling across this sharply contoured forest, is Poppy Hills, the only golf course on the Monterey Peninsula that is entirely inland. Looming on all sides are the thick, impenetrable woodlands. Tall, straight pines crowd closely together, cloaking the scene with a darkening silence. Here and there are gleaming cypress glades and thickets of crouching, twisted live oaks. It is, said Robert Louis Stevenson, the kind of wood for murderers to crawl among." The terrain is pitched and rolling, so hilly that one

might easily imagine oneself in the mountains or foothills of North Carolina. One fellow who played the course recently said that if they flattened all the hills, it might occupy more territory than any course in California.

Poppy Hills has the distinction of being the only course in the United States to be developed, owned and operated by an amateur golf association. The proprietor in this case is the Northern California Golf Association, a regional organization of some three hundred clubs that has more than 170,000 members. I suppose that no other golf club in this United States is larger than this. In the early 1970s, the association was showing signs of outgrowing the lease arrangement it had with Pebble Beach Company for the use of Spyglass Hill, and began to think seriously about developing its own facility. The association had grown to nearly 100,000 members, and

they were an active lot who believed that any reason was a good reason to organize a competition. In 1987 alone, the association staged ninety tournaments, covering 170 tournament days, at Poppy Hills.

The strain of competition runs deep in this region, which has produced some of America's finest players. With them came a tradition of strong leaders who found in the game sufficient reason to spread its values, and the satisfactions of competition, to players of all levels. Charles Seaver is one of these men. At the age of nineteen, Seaver went to the semifinals of the 1930 U.S. Amateur Championship at Merion, where he lost on the thirty-sixth hole to Gene Homans, the man Bobby Jones beat the next day to finish off his historic Grand Slam. Two years later, Seaver was a member of the Walker Cup team that defeated Great Britain at Broookline. The American side included Don Moe, Jess Sweetser, George Dunlap, Francis Ouimet, Gus Moreland and George Voight, who were then the cream of the world's amateurs. One of the things Seaver remembers most about the matches was the impression left on the Walker Cup by Leonard Crawley, one of his opponents. Crawley, who became one of the leading golf journalists of his

day, was a wold-class cricket player and an aggressive, rambunctious golfer. The impression Seaver refers to is a dent left in the silver Walker Cup trophy, which happened to be resting alongside the green, by Crawley's second shot on the eighteenth hole. The dent is there today.

Seaver won every California amateur championship at least once during the early 1930s, played nationally for four years and then went quietly and successfully into business in Fresno. He continued to play, sometimes in competition but mostly for enjoyment, and took an active interest in the affairs of the Northern California Golf Association. Seaver had learned the game from his father, Everett Seaver, who had won the Trans-Mississippi Amateur title in 1908 and remained a top amateur for many years. They played at Los Angeles Country Club, whose North Course is one of America's greatest tests of golf; one that has never held the U.S. Open, but should.

Charley inherited more than a love for the game from his father. He could play. In 1927, when Charley was sixteen, the Seavers met in the first round of the California Amateur Championship. Charley won. "I didn't want to, but I did. We were very, very competi-

tive," Seaver recalls. The love of competition was and still is a strong part of the Seaver family ethic. You can see it in Charley's own son, Tom, who probably won't contend for the U.S. Amateur golf title next year but who had the talent and the heart to become one of the great major-league pitchers of his generation. In the Seaver family, everyone had to earn his mark. You learned to do the best you could.

When Charley was fifteen, he accompanied his father to Cypress Point, where Alister MacKenzie was putting the finishing touches on his newest design. MacKenzie was a good friend of Everett Seaver's and wanted to see how his course would measure up to high standards of play. "I think we were the first persons to play Cypress Point," Seaver says today. "I had five straight birdies from the fourth through the eighth holes, and shot 76. Dr. MacKenzie seemed very pleased. Back then, I didn't think golf was hard." At age seventy-seven, Seaver knows better. He had managed to beat his age more than once, an accomplishment he is proud of, but no prouder than he is of the creation of Poppy Hills. Seaver is one of a group of directors on the Northern California Golf Association, all ex-presidents, who were determined to establish a

Behind the bunkers, shown above, that guard a tiny corner of the huge fourth green, lies the "Swale of Regret," a villainous hollow that is all but hidden on the left. The seventeenth green is shown on page 84.

permanent home for the association. The group included men like Francis Watson, a San Francisco lawyer; Bob Foley, an attorney from Albany; Charles Van Ling, a Palo Alto stockbroker; Ledlie Blue, a Sanger businessman and Richard Ghent of Pebble Beach, an automobile dealer. They built up a large treasure chest by tacking on a surcharge each year to members' handicap cards. In 1977, they had enough to enter into a purchase agreement with Pebble Beach Company for 168 acres of Del Monte Forest land. It took seven years to pay off the $1.5 million purchase price. In the meantime, the association needed someone to steer the project through the difficult permitting process, which in California can be an excruciating experience, and to organize a sound, profitable golf operation. The man they turned to was John Zoller, who was brought on board in 1979.

Zoller is just the sort of fellow you would want for the job. He was one of the earliest in a long line of great players developed by coach Bob Keppler at Ohio State University, playing number one on the team in the mid 1940s after service in World War II. Zoller, now in his early seventies, is the kind of player who likes hitting a one-iron and still carries a handicap of one. He is a man who enjoys playing the game for its own sake, yet he derives as much satisfaction from tending and nurturing a golf course as he does from playing it. This led Zoller into a long and distinguished career in turfgrass golf operations and country club management. After many years at the Eugene Country Club in Oregon, Zoller came to the Monterey Peninsula Country Club as greenkeeper and then general manager. He moved on to Pebble Beach Company as Director of Golf Operations before joining the Northern California Golf Association as its chief executive officer.

Five years later, in 1984, the permitting process was completed. It was time to build the golf course. The man chosen to design it was Robert Trent Jones, Jr., and two years later, on June 1, 1986, Poppy Hills opened. The site had quite enough natural difficulty, so there was no need to create more. "When we got into the property, we found the contours were even more severe than the topographic maps showed. We actually had to ease them," Jones says. In designing the course, Jones had to juggle several objectives laid down by Zoller and the association. Poppy Hills would serve as a tournament course for official events and thus would have

The first hole, at right, curls downhill, its fairway divided into strategic patches by cross-rough and bunkers.

On pages 90–91, is the long sixteenth which plays across two barrancas, enclosed on all sides by the impenetrable woodland, the kind for "murderers to crawl among."

to be of championship caliber. It would also have to be a course where NCGA members could play every day, and it would have to be adaptable for women. Finally, because it would be operated as a public course to satisfy profit expectations, it would have to be a course that could stand up to heavy play. With so many masters to serve the design would have to exhibit a high degree of flexibility.

What emerged was a course of deep complexity, with a rich structure of golfing strategies and situations. It almost seems to unfold in layers, presenting you with a series of options that may shift according to the temper of the day or the mood of the moment.

"We put a lot of golf in this course, because it isn't on the sea and because the client needed a course of championship caliber," Jones says. To achieve the flexibility and complexity he wanted, Jones has incorporated four basic design treatments into the layout: large greens, novel bunkering patterns, split fairways and multiple tees that vary the lengths of the holes as much as forty to fifty yards for men, and an average of eighty to one hundred yards per hole for women, even on certain par threes. In the main, the greens are a good deal larger than the

proportions of the holes might suggest, but these huge putting surfaces, some of which are 120 feet across, are the design elements that were probably most important in creating the kind of adaptability Jones and Zoller were seeking.

"We start with the idea that large greens are more practical and useful where the course is subjected to heavy traffic," says Jones. "But more to the point, people think that the target in golf is the green. It's not. The hole is the target. So building large greens is not necessarily an evil. If one can accept that, then one can break the green into two or three different areas, quite separate from one another, which is the key to providing a variety of golfing options." This creates a multitude of angles from which the target can be attacked, which is the basic thread Jones has used in weaving an intricate structure of golfing situations into the fabric of the course.

To make the large greens palatable, Jones has designed them so that they will gather shots. He has shaped them like saucers, higher at the edges, so that the ball will work toward the center of the putting surfaces. The complexity builds as one moves away from the greens because of the structure of the fairways. Jones has divided the

fairways, in effect, into strategic bits and pieces using cross-hazards, center bunkering that angles across fairways, and crossing rough. The result of playing to these multiple targets is that the holes can be approached from a variety of positions and angles. Thus, on many of the holes, there is not necessarily a correct way to play for advantage. Instead, you have a choice of routes, any one of which will get you home in time for dinner. All you have to do is hit the right shots. It is positional golf of the highest order, the epitome of the aerial game.

Byron Nelson once said that there are only two problems in golf, distance and direction, and I can't argue with logic like that. Two things strike me, though, as setting professional players apart from the rest of us. First, the pros can putt. Secondly, they know how far they hit with each club—not just in general, but precisely. When Greg Norman says it is 137.5 yards to the front of the cup, he is not just blowing froth from a Foster's. He knows how to hit that shot. This is a skill needed for the aerial game—indeed it is the culmination of a long breeding process with the pros, like racehorses bred to go a mile and one-eighth. It is a skill that is honed on American style

The first par three has two distinctly different putting surfaces,
that are guarded by bunkers on the left and back right
plus a deep ravine that has to be carried.

courses, and it is why so many American pros are uncomfortable on the British links. When you have mastered this skill, there tends to be a touch of outrage and dismay if a perfectly planned, perfectly executed stroke goes awry. This is an attitude that has been around American golf for a long time and I do not think it has ever been any stronger than it is now. For this reason, I think Poppy Hills will turn out to be an immensely popular course because it is a fascinating and powerful expression of the American style of golf architecture. The tone is established on the first hole, where the need for positional play is put to you with stunning clarity. The fairway falls away to the right, curling downhill with a dark, ominous ravine flanking the entire length of the hole, drawing you into its gathering gloom. Bunkers and cross-rough separate the fairway, and you can either lay up on the left side or go for a big drive along the right. Either way, you are assured of an approach shot to a green that lies below you. Which mood are you in? This is much too stern for an opening hole because of the frightening gulch on the slicers' side, but golf, like politics, ain't beanbag.

In spite of the emphasis on aerial golf, many of the holes,

beginning with the third, are open at the front to allow weaker players to bump the ball onto the green. The greens are Pencross Bent, and Zoller keeps them fast. The rough are planted in rye, the fairways in Colonial Bent. If Zoller can keep Poa annua the dominant turfgrass on the peninsula, from this course, he will be reckoned a proper wizard because no one else has managed to do so. The fairway targets are relatively large and wide, a feature for which the higher-handicap player will be grateful. From the forward tees, access to the fairways looks to be fair and reasonable.

The ninth hole approaches the ultimate in strategic complexity, positional golf carried to the extreme. There are more options here than on the Chicago futures market. It is as bewildering as a hall of mirrors, especially at first sight. How does one explain a hole that offers two sets of tees, both set deep in the woods and each playing from a different direction? A mountainous center bunkering hazard stretches across the fairway at an angle, beyond which is a plateau. The fairway islands are set at angles to one another on this long par five. Once up on the plateau—two shots for most of us—here is an approach across a steeply banked ravine to a long,

long green. The ravine has been cleared of brush, but this has been replaced with long, thick ryegrass rough, so landing there is hardly a Sunday afternoon picnic. Long hitters will try to make the green in two strokes, and some will succeed, but they will have to be terrific blows, and straight.

Did I say the green was long? Well, I tried to pace it off and had to stop for lunch. Think of a highway, or rather a freeway. It lacks only a toll booth. I can easily imagine some players who will need an eight iron to get from front to back. One can play this hole, and probably should, from point to point, sneaking up on it like an Apache stalking a lone bison. Bring big arrows for that final shot, though.

A road bisects the property so that there are eleven holes on one side and seven on the other. The only odd feature of the design is that the back nine has three par fives and three par threes. The reason for this is the way the land was shaped. It worked out better that way on the land we found, Jones says. "I was more interested in the holes working well than in being rigidly orthodox." In fact, the sequence of the back nine flows smoothly. At the twelfth, there is a grove of dwarf cypress that Jones was determined to save because it

Many of the green entrances, like the eighth,
have been left open at the front to allow players
to bump the ball onto the spacious putting surfaces.

Number ten, a par five of 510 yards,
shown above from the landing area towards
the green, and from behind the green
in the photograph at right.

is a species that was discovered by Sam Morse. The hole doglegs sharply around the grove and Jones has inserted some Florida-style bunkers at the turn that even Fred Couples couldn't carry. Jones hopes that this will keep long hitters from trampling through the fragile dwarf cypress while searching for lost golf balls. These bunkers, considered by many as too penal, have been significantly cut back in size, but still steering the players away from the dwarf cypress.

There are two ponds on the golf course, entering play on just three holes. On both ponds Jones has fashioned little wooden platforms from which native water plants grow. These are actually little fortresses for the ducks that live in the ponds, designed so that other animals cannot steal their eggs. For a course that is so completely enclosed by forest, Jones has given us a remarkable variety of visual impressions and has kept the trees far enough away from the playing areas that we do not eel cramped. At the fourth hole, a long par five, he swings its double-dogleg fairway in a natural and very appealing way toward bunkers that are visually graceful and strategically wicked. Every leading authority agrees that humongous is not a word, but the green here is just

humongous, measuring in excess of ten thousand square feet. In back, piercing into the left side of the green is a villainous hollow, rather like a reverse Valley of Sin but hidden shamefully, a place I shall think of, forevermore, as the Swale of Regret.

An entirely different look is presented at the sixteenth hole, a long par four that curves majestically to the right and plays across two barrancas. The tee shot must carry the first, which has been left in wasteland and has the look of Pine Valley. The second ravine is manicured but deep, and you are looking down slightly at a dish-shaped green with bunkers left and right. A strong and vivid hole.

Temptation is something few golfers can resist, and never more than when it seems just within reach. Poppy Hills is full of temptations, large and small, beckoning from nearly every corner. Jack Guio, who was the personable head professional at Poppy Hills during 1982, offers this insight: "The great problem on this course is that it dangles realistic chances in front of you, but you don't dare miss. If you do miss a shot, you probably won't get away with a bogey. You can look for some big numbers, certainly doubles and maybe triples. Satan must have a

branch office around here somewhere, because there's a lot of temptation on this course. And you'd better be prepared to think of the consequences first, before you hit it."

The competitive course record of 70 is held by Brian Watts, the 1987 NCAA champion from Oklahoma State, recorded during the matches held between the NCAA All-Americans and a team from Japan in 1987.

The name Poppy Hills is unusual, especially to those from outside California, and has given rise to an occasional barb of sly humor. When Dave Marr, the glib and irreverent ABC-TV commentator, heard about it, he asked in his Texas drawl, "Do you guys in California still smoke the divots?" As a matter of fact, Poppy Hills got its name in a perfectly honorable way. It is named for the golden poppy, the official flower of the state of California, which the Northern California Golf Association adopted as its symbol when the group was formed in 1903.

The association has grown from five original member clubs to more than 300, with another 360 associated club organizations. Which of those early members could have imagined the enormous growth of the game, and who

The thirteenth, completely surrounded by the ever present forest is a par four, 393 yards long, whose green is guarded by two bunkers on the right.

among them could have dreamed that one day the Northern California Golf Association would command the resources to own and operate a modern golf facility like Poppy Hills? One wonders if other golf associations will follow. There have been hints recently that the Southern California and Massachusetts Golf Associations are planning similar projects. Nothing is more needed in the game today, and nowhere is there a better example of how the idea can be made to work. The NCGA has since completed a second course called Poppy Ridge, which was designed by Rees Jones. Bobby Jones' brother.

As for the golf, Poppy Hills has a personality and a presence unlike any of the other courses on the Monterey Peninsula. It will energize your game, or plunge it to despair. It will invite transgression, then treat you with scorn. It will promise and bewitch, and then hold you for the contemptible pretender that you are. And if, at the end of the round, you feel a sense of well-being and satisfaction, you can be sure that, on that day, the head was on straight and the swing was responding with assurance and ease. In any case, you might want to remember that the most important distance in golf is the one you find between your ears.

In the late afternoon, as shadows lengthen across the eighteenth fairway,
Poppy Hills turns a final, welcoming face toward those who have challenged—
a bewitching invitation to return.

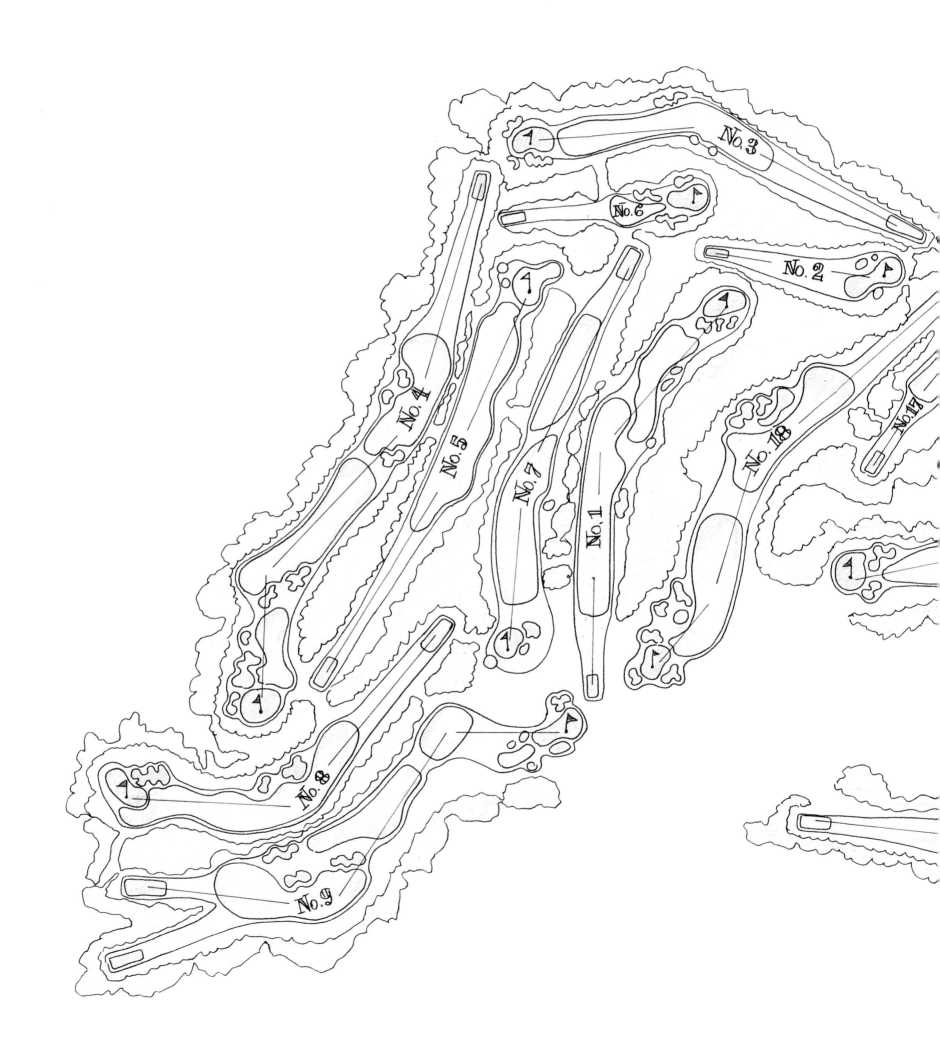

POPPY HILLS GOLF COURSE

COURSE RATING: 75.0

HOLE	1	2	3	4	5	6	7	8	9		10	11	12	13	14	15	16	17	18		
PAR	4	3	4	5	4	3	4	4	5	36	5	3	5	4	4	34	3	5	5	36	72
YARDS	413	162	406	560	426	181	388	380	557	3,473	510	214	531	393	417	210	439	163	500	3,377	6,850

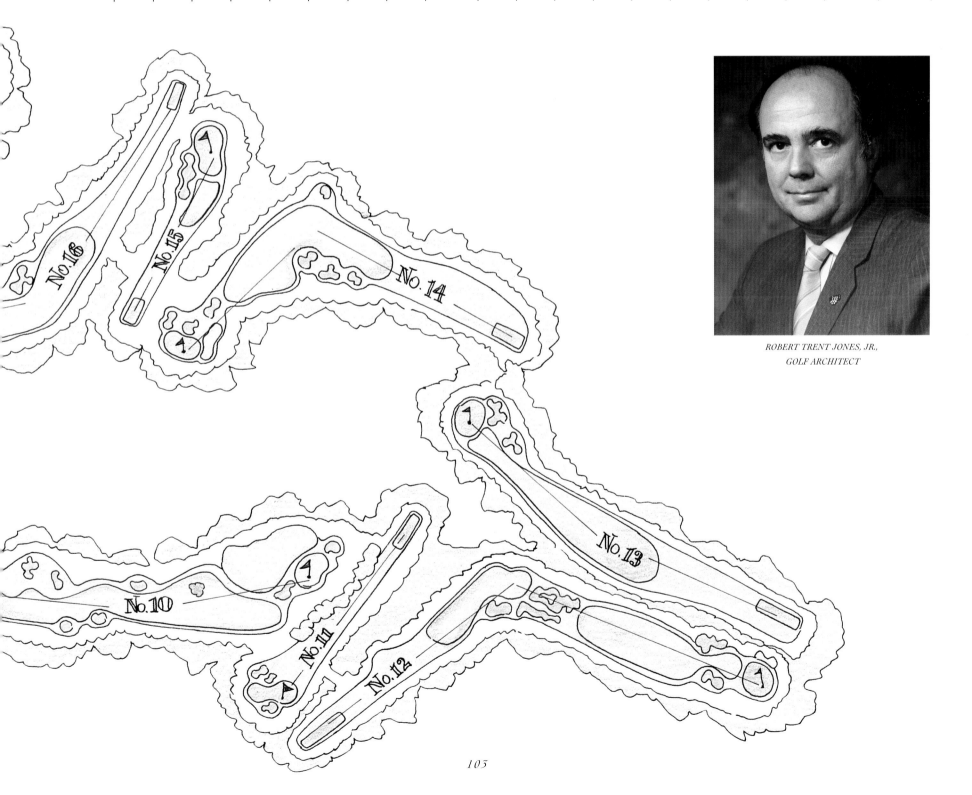

ROBERT TRENT JONES, JR.,
GOLF ARCHITECT

Monterey Peninsula Country Club

*O*NE DAY A MAN STEPPED TO the tee of the 335 yard ninth hole at the Monterey Peninsula Country Club, leaned his sturdy frame into the shot and drove his ball onto the green. He wasn't even angry. He was Lawson Little.

During the mid 1930s and early 1940s Lawson Little had won two United States Amateur and two British Amateur Championships and then as a professional, the National Open, as it was called in those days. Little was a great player whose game was marked by exceptional length, so it was not especially surprising that he could drive the ninth hole, although it is one of those stories people like to tell around the club. The point of retelling it here is that Little had traveled all over the world, had enjoyed great success and celebrity and could have settled almost anywhere when his competitive days were over. But he chose to retire at the the Monterey

Peninsula Country Club. It was a place where Little enjoyed playing the game in a setting he loved.

Little lived off the sixth tee overlooking a ravine in a house that Jimmy Demaret called Gibson Gulch, after Little's favorite drink. He would see the country club grow into a large operation, a bustling place with two eighteen-hole golf courses, but in those days there was only one.

The original course, the second-oldest on the Monterey Peninsula, was named the Dunes Course. It is not as punishing as Pebble Beach nor as artful a creation as Cypress Point because it is laid out in gentler terrain. But there is a naturalness about it that suggests a link with the golf of an earlier age. As I strolled some of the holes, particularly those near the ocean, I could not help but think of a passage written by Arnold Haultain, a golfer of the era. In his marvelous book, *The Mystery of Golf,* a book

that belongs in every golfer's library, he wrote: "How beautiful the vacated links at dawn, when the dew gleams untrodden beneath the pendant flags and the long shadows lie quietly on the greens, when no one intrudes upon the still and silent lawns and you stroll from hole to hole and drink in the beauties of a land to which you know you will be all too blind when the sun mounts high and you toss for the honor."

It is the kind of beauty that emerges from the form of nature. There is evidence that Seth Raynor, who designed the course, had a feel for the natural line because he had produced several earlier courses much admired for this quality, among them Fisher's Island in New York, the Country Club of Fairfield, Connecticut and Yeaman's Hall in Charleston, South Carolina. The terrain for the Monterey Peninsula course is a mixture of hilly, forested inland shapes and open ground that flattens toward the sea. When you consider that the sole purpose of the golf course was to provide attractive frontage for real estate lots, the first such development in the United States, it is apparent that Raynor was a gifted and resourceful man. The course wanders through the forest, where the homesites are concentrated, then moves out to the ocean through the middle holes and returns through the woods and ravines to the clubhouse.

The opening holes are laid into the contours of the terrain with a wonderful ease, with few of the sudden, artificial intrusions that so often are forced into an uneven landscape. The holes are arranged in such a way that when ravines, barrancas and other irregularities occur, they seem to appear logically and naturally in the scheme of things. The golf is of a very testing order that is generous to a well-played shot and gives a poor stroke what it deserves.

These are qualities that are genuinely admired by those who enjoy the game most when it is least pretentious in putting the challenge. Dave Marr and Ed Sneed are great admirers of the Dunes Course. Gene Littler once said that the first twelve holes of this course are as fine a stretch of consecutively good holes as he has played. Bill Erwin, a former president of the club, says that "The front nine looks easy but it isn't. I don't know much about golf courses, but that opening nine is just unbeatable. It's a delight for us amateurs because it has so much character."

Rock outcroppings split the fairway on the panoramic thirteenth of the Shore Course at right, and tumble down to the edge of the large, tilting green.

The inland holes are generally tight, and the greens run to the smallish side with subtle rather than severe breaks. There is an old-fashioned flavor to the greens that one hopes will not be changed by a future Green Committee. One is careful not to overshoot these greens because behind them the ground is all unkempt rough, bushes and trees.

Raynor died before completing the course. The few holes that remained were finished by Robert Hunter, with the collaboration of Alister MacKenzie, and the course opened in 1925. Hunter followed Raynor's general plan, and there is evidence of MacKenzie's work among the dunes holes, at greens like the tenth and twelfth.

Although the seaside holes have the appearance of the links style, they are not a true links because the fairways are generously supplied with water. Beginning at the thirteenth hole, the course opens onto a wide vista leading to Point Joe, a treacherous shoal that juts into the restless sea. Several ocean currents converge at this point in a turbulent swell that is said to have caused many shipwrecks. Just there, at the apex of Point Joe, is the fourteenth hole, a par three that is completely bare and open to the elements. Rarely

The solitary fourteenth of the Dunes Course is approached across the serpentine lines of this bunker, fully exposed to the elements beside the restless sea.

does it play to its length of 159 yards as winds change its conditions almost by the hour and one is as apt to be playing a short iron as a long wood.

To the left of the thirteenth fairway is an open field that is used as a practice ground. It faces across the flattened dunes to the ocean, surely one of the world's most glorious settings for discovering the latest secret of golf. Regrettably, this is an experience that can be enjoyed only by its members because the Monterey Peninsula Country Club guards its privacy well. Its membership of about 750 is an active one; golf director Bob Holmes reports that sixty-three thousand rounds are played each year over the club's two courses. For years, the Monterey Peninsula Country Club was just abut the best bargain in golf and, as things have turned out, maybe the best bargain in the history of private clubs.

When the course was built, Morse wanted to surround it with moderately priced real estate lots, a key part of his plan to develop the Monterey peninsula. But it didn't catch on; an economic depression was on the way and for years Morse struggled to keep the club alive. Dues were $5 per month, scarcely a token, because Morse and his

company were willing to underwrite the operating expenses for the club and the course. For thirty years Morse tried to sell the club to the members but each of his proposals was met with a firm rejection. The membership could discern no logical reason to pay for something that was being supplied so satisfactorily. Once, in 1948, the members were asked for a modest increase in dues, from $5 to $8, but this suggestion was crushed. These were prickly times, but with the infusion of newer members sentiment began to change, and by the late 1950s it looked as though the membership might accept Morse's offer. He would sell the club and its 422 acres for the grand sum of one dollar, with the stipulation that the members would agree to build a second course.

For a while there it looked like a close call but someone coughed up a buck and the acquisition was completed in 1959. The second course followed in less than two years. Bob Baldock was hired to design and build the course, which opened in 1961 and was named the Shore Course. A curious and somewhat wistful historical note is that Alister MacKenzie had been asked by Sam Morse to design the Shore Course in 1927,

while he was working on Cypress Point, and apparently he completed a preliminary routing plan. Unfortunately, hard economic times intervened, but just imagine a MacKenzie course on that beckoning terrain.

Baldock was a former professional golfer who had been a construction man for architect Billy Bell, and he went on to design many courses in California and the Southwest. Strangely, both Jack Neville and Lawson Little were members of the club but neither seems to have been consulted on the design of the Shore Course.

It is laid out in a similar pattern to the Dunes Course, starting and finishing in the wooded area at the clubhouse, but it has more holes in the open dunesland adjacent to the ocean. This puts it more in the elements, which may account for the fact that the fairways are wider than those of the Dunes Course. There are fewer forced carries as well, which may be a boon to the higher-handicap player. The greens on the Shore Course are large and undulating, which makes it a tougher putting course than the Dunes. "You have to hit the ball underneath the hole unless you want to three-putt all day," observes Bob Hanna, a longtime member. Many of the greens are slanted into the fairways, creating a

At dusk, a lone golfer faces across the flattened linksland
alongside the thirteenth fairway,
a memorable setting for the practice ground.

diverse and sometimes bewildering array of approach shots. The bunkers guarding many of the greens are set a distance away from the putting surfaces, a treatment favored by a golf architect named Robert Bruce Harris. He had designed many courses in the Midwest and the South with this feature because he believed it to be a maintenance-saving device. Harris was brought in to modify the Shore Course in 1962. His revisions to the bunkering, and other changes at six of the holes, were completed in 1963. The Monterey Peninsula Country Club has hosted several well-known tournaments, including two Senior Women's Amateur Championships in 1968 and 1976, the Trans-Mississippi Amateur in 1956, and a two-day television match in 1959 in which Dutch Harrison beat Jack Fleck and Ken Venturi. And it was part of the original rotation for the Bing Crosby tournament. In the early days, when the tournament was a three-day event, the entire field played Cypress Point on Friday, Monterey Peninsula on Saturday and finished at Pebble Beach on Sunday. The Clambake Dinner became a tradition at the country club, featuring a Calcutta pool, more or less legal in those days, and the usual pretournament non-

sense. Crosby and Demaret would sing, sometimes with unsolicited help. Jimmy Durante would entertain, mortally wounding the club's piano. Venturi and Harvie Ward, the amateur wonder boys, would perform soft shoe. Bets would be laid that no one could drink Peter Hay, the giant Scottish pro at Pebble Beach, under the table (nobody could). Phil Harris would attempt to restore order, and old-timers recall seeing Sam Morse who was about five feet eight, bulling his way through the crowd with Tarzan (Johnny Weissmuller) on his shoulders.

Those days, sadly, have passed and in 1967 the country club course passed from the tournament's rotation, replaced with Spyglass Hill. Other traditions were passing, too. One of these was the 'gang-some,' an amiable and particularly virile form of golf in which an indeterminate number of players assault the course en masse, as many as eight or ten, or more, playing the holes together. In gangsome golf, an elevensome is perfectly acceptable and proper. The gangsome idea was not invented at Monterey Peninsula, but it was probably perfected here. One of the regulars was Warner Keeley. "We would have anywhere from seven to fourteen players and we

The ninth hole of the Dunes Course, at right, is a beautifully shaped, shortish par five that leads toward the sea, whose murmuring sounds echo along the tree-lined corridor.

The windswept green at the par three tenth hole of the Dunes Course, shown on pages 114–115, is laid into the rolling dunesland with a wonderful ease—much easier on the eyes than on the nerves.

were all good players so we could get around the course in three hours, sometimes less. The betting would get pretty intricate. What games they were," Keeley recalls with some relish. Another participant was F.A. 'Buck' Henneken, a perennial club champion, who provides further elaboration: "Actually, we'd have twelve to sixteen players in the mornings; in the afternoon there would only be ten or twelve. Yeah, we'd go around in three hours, easy. And walking, too. The foursomes ahead of us used to hold us up. They would be frantic, trying to keep out of our way. They couldn't stand the idea of letting a gangsome play through."

The gangsomes are outlawed now, a victim of the inevitable growth of the game and the order it now imposes, or perhaps of a tamer breed of men. Every so often, late in the day, they say that you can still see an occasional fivesome on the course. Maybe this is a grudging or graceful nod to a dying tradition. Men like Henneken and Keeley might chuckle when they remember that, in the old days, a fivesome was something a gangsome was waiting to play through.

But some traditions have survived, not all of them on the golf course. Next to golf, according to the club's official history, the oldest tradition of the club is the men's card room where legends lurk in every corner. Here lifelong friendships are made and kept. Feuds are begun and never ended. Fortunes are won and lost, at all hours of the day and night.

The club has also established new traditions. As the membership grew, it became obvious that something would have to be done to regulate starting times during periods of heavy play. A simple solution was devised. Reservations were taken for every other time slot on the starting sheet; the tee times in between were left open for any members who could present a foursome at the first tee, ready to play. It was a popular innovation, and eminently sensible. Eventually, it would be copied by many other clubs.

The Spanish Colonial-style clubhouse sits among the trees, approached by a long driveway that rises to the summit of a tall hill. Morse had a great fondness for trees. When the clubhouse was built, he allowed only enough to be felled to leave space for the building. This insistence on preserving sylvan beauty created awkward parking arrangements, especially when, as the club historian notes, the tall shadows of the pines mixed

Barrancas, ravines and tiny brooks appear naturally in the layout of the inland holes of the Dunes Course, at top right, as in this well-proportioned hazard on the approach to the fourth hole, a short par four.

At bottom right, the most frequent visitors to the course, and constant companions.

with fog and grog, especially at night. It was on just such a night that Morse, emerging from a late dinner celebration, got tangled up in the maze and banged his car on a tree. Early the next morning a crew arrived to remove most of the trees."

Morse always showed a stubborn determination when it came to preserving the natural assets of his domain. Bing Crosby once described it as "an almost religious devotion." But Bing admired this deeply. "I shall never cease being grateful to him for that, because without Sam Morse the Monterey Peninsula would all be Coney Island," Crosby said.

Morse was shrewd as well as stubborn. "Our most precious asset here is not so much the land itself," he said, "it is the beauty of the land." It is the kind of beauty that people continue to find irresistible, and is probably the reason people like Lawson Little chose to live here.

Those of us who cannot live here try to return as often as we can. Mike Souchak is one of those who does. Souchak, who tore up the professional tour a generation or so after Lawson Little did, now lives in Florida where he runs a business, competes now and then on the Senior Tour and presides

over one of the finest private collections of vintage wine in America.

"Every summer, we take a house at the Country Club," Souchak says. "We bring the whole family and spend the month of August. It's so much fun playing golf there, and I just love the Dunes Course. It's not a killer, but it is a great test of golf. The course changes constantly because of all the elements. It's a wonderful place for anybody to come, and for a golfer it's the greatest place in the world."

A panoramic view of the Shore Course looks southward across the open terrain that slopes from the forest toward the rumbling ocean. In the background is the faint outline of the dunes at Spyglass Hill Golf Course.

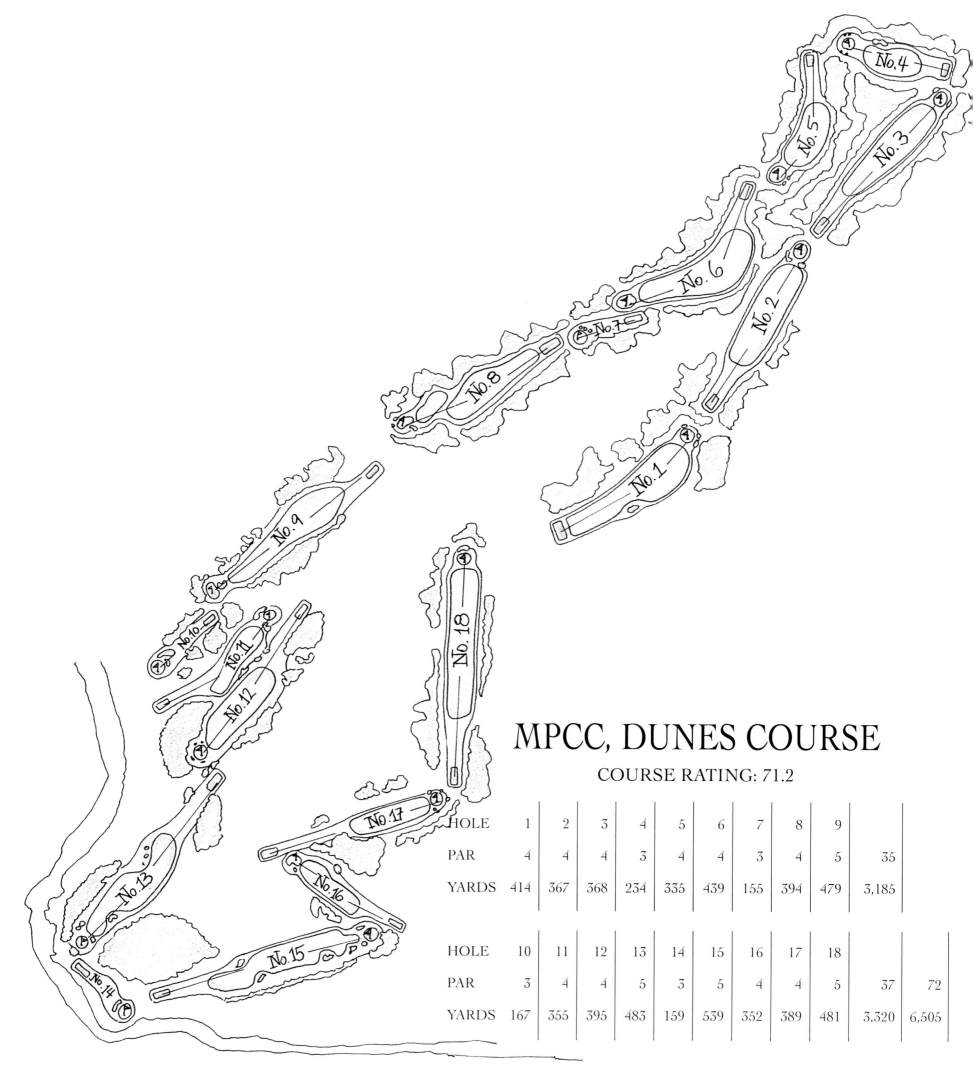

MPCC, DUNES COURSE

COURSE RATING: 71.2

HOLE	1	2	3	4	5	6	7	8	9	
PAR	4	4	4	3	4	4	3	4	5	35
YARDS	414	367	368	234	335	439	155	394	479	3,185

HOLE	10	11	12	13	14	15	16	17	18		
PAR	3	4	4	5	3	5	4	4	5	37	72
YARDS	167	355	395	483	159	539	352	389	481	3,320	6,505

MPCC, SHORE COURSE

COURSE RATING: 70.5

HOLE	1	2	3	4	5	6	7	8	9		10	11	12	13	14	15	16	17	18		
PAR	5	4	3	4	4	4	3	4	5	36	3	5	3	4	5	3	4	4	4	35	71
YARDS	485	377	149	364	370	349	222	363	502	3,181	153	506	183	428	538	165	394	349	446	3,126	6,343

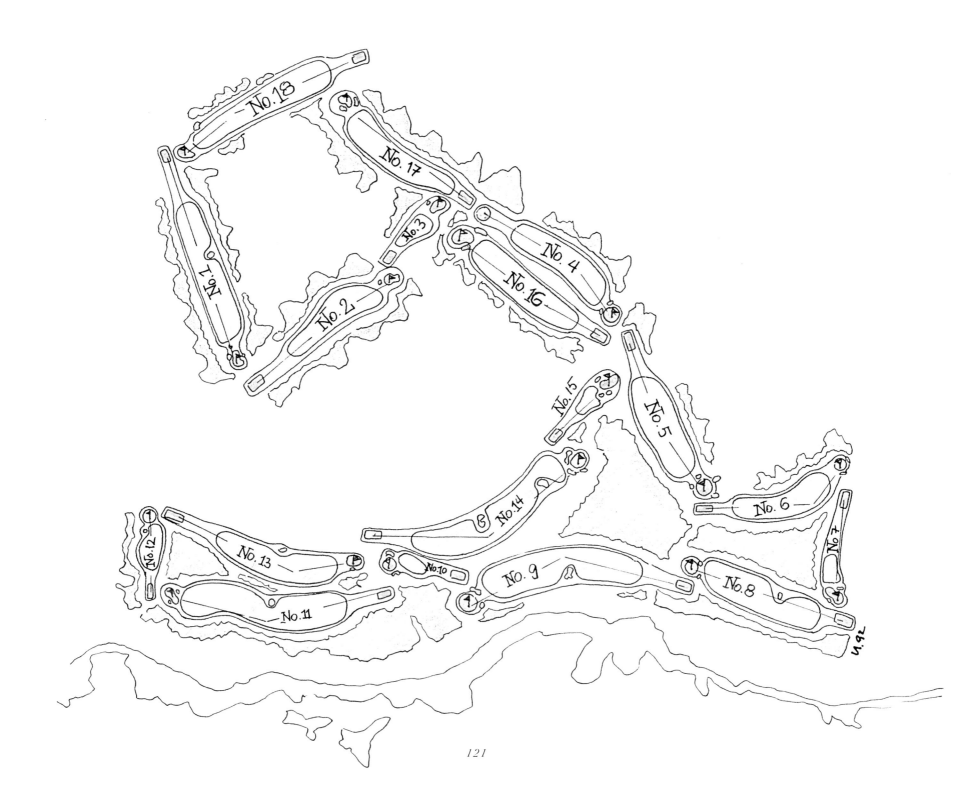

The Links at Spanish Bay

*I*T IS TO THE LINKSLAND THAT golfers are most happily and inexorably drawn, and why should it not be so; because it is from linksland that the game arose. In the earliest days, the somewhat belligerent and hardy folk who inhabited Scotland discovered that the most suitable playing ground for this pastime was the sandy wasteland beside the sea where the ground was wide open and needn't be tended. This probably appealed to the practical Scots, but more to the point it was a setting that shaped the way in which the game evolved.

Learning to cope with the rough elements and the uncertainties of terrain was accepted as a natural part of the game and supplied much of its satisfaction. It was a game in which man was exposed to the forces and whims of nature, a pure and direct confrontation in which he had to rely entirely on his own resources. The best man was not always the strongest or the bravest among them; cunning and guile counted for something. Luck did not always favor the most resourceful man, but that, too, was understood to be in the scheme of things. All that the game has become, its ethos, its strategies, its refinements, its substance, evolved slowly and gradually on these early links in places like Leith, Perth and St. Andrews and gave to the game its essential character. Later, as the game spread to other regions of Scotland and then England, these linksland settings were repeated at places like Dornoch, Prestwick, North Berwick, Hoylake, Muirfield and Troon. To this day, the British hold firmly to the belief that only a linksland course can provide a complete test of championship golf, which is why there are no inland courses in the British Open rota.

Although we have grown accustomed to it, it seems strange that America has

taken so long to produce a single
golf course that can be called a true
links. There is a links flavor to
some of our earliest courses, like
The National and Shinnecock Hills
on Long Island, and there are
snatches of linksland on the Outer
Banks of North Carolina, at
courses like Kittansett and Hyannis-
port in Massachusetts, and more
recently, at Wild Dunes in South
Carolina. American golf grew up
around large metropolitan centers
like Chicago, Philadelphia and
New York where linksland does
not exist. The inland, parkland setting of their courses gave rise to a
different, more formal and highly
crafted sole of golf architecture
that began in England but reached
its greatest expression in America.
As a consequence, the game that
emerged in America gradually took
on a different character. In many
ways, it was a more exacting form
of golf that carried with it subtle,
inevitable differences in how we
experienced the game and in our
attitudes toward it. There were seaside courses, to be sure, where the
terrors and excitement of wind and
weather could be fully experienced.
But, until now, none of these
courses had been laid out in the
kind of terrain in which the game
originated. This national omission
has been corrected now, with the

*A long view of the sixth hole,
at right, a lovely par four that
climbs between the bristly
wild grasses and a series
of gentle humps.*

*Golf arose in Scotland on the
sandy wasteland beside the sea, a
setting for golf that finally has
reached American shores, as the
view of the sixth hole on
pages 126 – 127 suggests.*

appearance of a proper links course at Spanish Bay.

Curiously it has taken us just one hundred years to do so; rudimentary holes for the first permanent golf club in the United States were laid out in John Reid's pasture in Yonkers, New York, in 1888.

Spanish Bay is a breathtaking new resort developed by Pebble Beach Company, a place that has become famous for its luxurious 270-room inn, its luxurious accommodations and its luxurious prices. It occupies the site of an old sand quarry that had been mined by Sam Morse to help pay for the upkeep of the Del Monte Forest. The huge natural dunes that once reached up to forty feet in height, where children used to play and slide, were nearly gone. In the old days, they were shipping out eight hundred to one thousand tons of sand a day, about twenty boxcars, to the glass and bottle plants in Northern California.

When Spanish Bay was built, truckloads of sand were moved back to replenish the terrain and rebuild the dunes. The golf course alone took nearly six hundred thousand cubic yards. The ground now slopes gradually to the sea over the reshaped contours of these dunes, with the golf holes folding across the rumpled terrain like a blanket.

The Links at Spanish Bay is the result of a collaboration among three men who have succeeded, against the odds, in producing a work of extraordinary charm and merit. Few courses that we now include in the first rank were, in their original form, the product of collaborations. Pine Valley and Augusta National are two that come to mind and, unless Pebble Beach Company has neither the wit nor the will to preserve it properly, Spanish Bay shows every promise of one day joining them. It has, I know, become as priceless an asset as any of the golfing jewels that adorn the Monterey Peninsula.

The collaboration at Spanish Bay were Robert 'Bobby' Jones, Jr., Frank B. 'Sandy' Tatum, and Tom Watson, who has managed to go through life without a nickname. Jones is an accomplished golf architect who spent a long apprenticeship with his famous father, with whom he collaborated on many courses. Later he established his own firm, which to date is responsible for more than sixty golf courses, most of them in the West and quite a few in some of the more exotic locales around the world.

Jones' taste for linksland golf was acquired gradually over a period of years. During the late 1970s

and early 1980s, he played increasingly in the British Isles and grew to like the freedom of the treeless courses and firm playing surfaces. "I learned how much fun it could be to use the air, to aim the ball wherever the conditions dictated and play according to feel. Instead of working mindlessly for a perfect swing, I was free to invent shots, both in the air and along the ground." These influences began showing up in his work and sharpened his eye for the technical details he knew would be needed to design a modern links.

Before Spanish Bay, neither Watson nor Tatum had been involved with the actual design of a golf course, although both men had taken a keen interest in the subject. Watson's had been shaped by his experiences in playing the British Open courses, where he had won five championships and developed an abiding affection for qualities of the game these courses evoked. Tatum is a lifelong amateur and a pillar of the United States Golf Association, which he once served as president with great distinction. Tatum had won the NCAA Championship in a year that I will have the kindness not to reveal, and after earning a law degree at Stanford had gone, as a Rhodes scholar, to Oxford and Cambridge

The eighteenth is a rough and rugged finishing hole,
surrounded by tangled sedges and gnarled bushes,
with a fearsome center hazard stretching toward the green.

in the days when Bernard Darwin still covered them, and he became deeply attached to the forms and attitudes of golf in the elements, British style. As these three men approached the Spanish Bay project, they had a clear idea of the role each would play. The general outline and routing plan was done by Jones. Tatum and Watson focused on the details and refinements that would introduce depth, subtlety and art into a given hole, with Watson providing the point of view of the professional player and Tatum the amateur viewpoint.

"In effect," Watson says, "Jones designed the canvas, while Tatum and I helped to paint it. The project intrigued me because I love links golf and it was a chance to design a links course in an area I love. One of the things that impresses me about the linksland courses in Britain is how well they are suited to the land. If you have real linksland, I don't think you need to put a lot of extra paint on the canvas"—Watson, the passionate professional.

Tatum, the passionate amateur: "Tom is very sensitive to golf course architecture, and I think I am. I have been fascinated by it almost all my life. Our common denominator in this project is our passion for the game. The process really involved digging, in our own ways, into the years each of us have devoted to the game and the feelings we have accumulated about golf holes that appeal to us and those that do not."

The interaction among the three was carried out on another level that contributed much to the texture of the design. Watson is a player and thus has learned to attack golf courses. "Watson has been an attacker all of his life," Jones says. "Mine has been spent trying to defend courses from these onslaughts. The collision of these two forces produces a creative tension that, when it is working well, can suggest better design solutions. Tatum has a superb evaluative eye, particularly for things that will not work, and he became the conscience of the design. As you might expect, his theories about the game have a sense of legal equity and so he would often be the judge. What made it work is that we all have respect for tradition and we like the natural game.

This love of the natural, linksland game led to a suggestion, first, and then a decision to plant fescue grass over the entire course, including the greens. Fescue is a cool-weather grass that forms the natural turf of the seaside courses in Britain and finishes much of the character of linksland golf. This was and probably still is a daring move because it had not been attempted here before. "Almost every agronomist we talked to, all over the country, warned us not to plant this course in fescue," Tatum recalls. "They said it was inferior to modern strains and would not heal as well. But the putting surfaces are so true, so completely free of grains, and the fairways are sensational.

Jones elaborates: "Fescue is bristly, stiff and very fine-bladed so the ball sits up. The great advantage of fescue, from the point of view of conservation, is that it needs very little water, about half the amount that other grasses require. The divot recovery is slower, but we provided for this by building wide fairways. The fescue turf will give Spanish Bay an entirely different look to those who are accustomed to playing over-watered, green fairways elsewhere. "We did not want that look at Spanish Bay," Watson explains. "The course will have a gray-green color during the winter and a dun color during he summer. That's the look of the links. Besides, if you over-water the fescue turf to make it green you destroy the character of the turf."

When Watson talks about this

The ninth hole, an uphill par four, has an element of mystery owing to the many folds and wrinkles introduced into the surface of the fairway.

character, he is talking about the feel of striking the ball from firm, tight fairways. Tatum takes this a step further. He talks about the sound. "There's a distinctive crunch that feels and sounds very special. It is a sound that is peculiar to fescue because of the way in which it knits. I've always loved that sound in playing links courses and I'm delighted that we could reproduce it here. It's a small thing, perhaps, but it adds significantly to the pleasure of playing links golf."

Think of it, the sound. We can agree that golf is a game of 'feel,' even a sensuous game in which the nerve endings sometimes respond in mysterious ways. We search for this feel constantly, and when we have it right, nothing is more satisfying. It is an elemental gratification, like a wolf sinking its teeth into a fresh kill. But here is a man talking about sound. This is a much subtler sensation. Who but a philosopher, or a skilled player whose strokes meet the turf with regular precision, would appreciate such a refinement?

As one explores the holes at Spanish Bay, one senses those traditional attitudes expressed by the designers and one can see the historical influences at work. The course opens toward the sea with a comfortable par five that slopes from the sand-colored Inn to a green that overlooks the ragged beach and pounding surf. The hole makes a gentle turn, just at the end, where a sandy wasteland guards the approach. You are into the heart of the linksland immediately, an altogether satisfying and urgent introduction. The second comes back uphill, one of those short par fours like the ninth at Cypress Point and tenth at Riviera that Watson has said he likes so well and wanted on this course. He found it here, a 307 yard climb to an elevated two-level green that rises in back, set into the large, unkempt dunes with the Inn and large cypress trees as a backdrop. It is full of the most wonderful sorts of mischief.

If the view from the third tee does not put you in a high spirit, then nothing will. From this vantage point at the crest of a dune, the linksland spreads out before you, unfurling to the ocean beyond. You could easily be in Dornoch, whose third hole was very much in the designers' minds when they built this one. The hole doglegs to the left, 405 yards, and its commanding view gives a wonderful sense of power that invites one to take a full bash. However, the hole is set up so that the green is easier to approach from the left side of

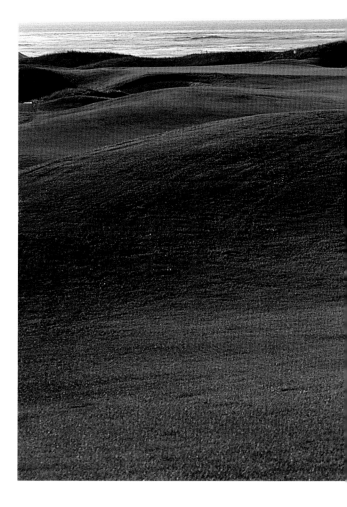

One can easily imagine how the elements could affect the game,
should Mother Nature decide to pay a visit.

the fairway, so the farther and safer you drive, the harder the second shot will be. There are probably better holes on the course, but none I would rather play. The fourth is a splendid one-shotter that fits into a natural saddle in the dunes, a setting that Robert Jones feels "was ordained by the Almighty."

The fifth is the first really big hole, a par four of 459 yards, and it introduces a theme, center bunkering, that will recur on other holes. Center bunkering is a strategic device whereby the bunkers are angled across the fairway at a diagonal. The farthest bunker is out of reach, the safe play. The shortest bunker can be carried, but it's risky. The center bunker, or bunkers, is within easy reach and is designed to catch drives aimed at the middle of the fairway. "This poses the risk versus reward options that are characteristic of links golf," Tatum says. "How you decide to play will depend on the conditions prevailing that day. It favors a thoughtful golfer who understands his limitations and has the sense to play within them."

There is more center bunkering at the sixth, an uphill par four that is beautifully set into the terrain. The green folds into a series of grass-covered bunkers that appear utterly natural—a lovely

hole. The seventh is a burly par four, with island fairways and forced carries across the wasteland, that moves downhill to the short eighth, a par three with a forced carry across the natural habitat, a sort of marsh with thick clumps of tall swamp grasses. This little hole parallels the ocean, from which the prevailing winds mutter on the right, and plays to a relatively wide, shallow green with bunkers behind. The ninth travels back uphill, a straightaway par four that ends at an elevated green. You'll want to spank the ball rather smartly here. Jones and his friends have introduced little wrinkles into the fairways, not everywhere, but often enough to raise suspicions that they are deliberate. Jones admits that they are, saying: "There should be some art and mystery in the game. The element of uncertainty, of the unexpected, is a part of links golf. Sometimes you will get an unfair bounce where a mediocre shot might reach the green, or a very good one might bounce into a bunker. That's the mystery." I believe it is fair to comment that the ninth hole has some mystery to it.

The first nine holes are laid entirely in the dunes, but at the start of the second nine there is a patch of holes along the road that

go through the trees, a necessary buffer between the Inn and the road. What could have been a sudden, unwelcome intrusion into the linksland motif is, in fact, a pleasing interlude that fits neatly into the rest of the course. What makes it work is a clever transition at the tenth hole, which starts in the dunes and finishes in the trees and the use of strong linksland themes in an inland setting where you might not expect to find them.

The tenth is a short par five that plays across a large, unruly dune from which a chunk has been gouged to create a blind shelf on the far side. There is a distinct advantage, and considerably more risk, in driving the ball to this shelf because it opens the hole quite nicely to the second shot and might even tempt a long hitter to have a go at the green. The second shot is played from the dunes setting into the trees, with the fairway rising to the green, past yet another cluster of center bunkers, and the transition seems as inevitable as it is natural. At the eleventh, a shortish par four that swings to the right, enough trees have been cleared to leave an open area on the left so that one does not feel enclosed in the forest, a nice visual touch and a sage direction in which to aim. But the hole is arranged in such a way

At the tenth hole there is a transition from the dunes to the distant trees, beginning a short stretch of inland holes.

that the approach to the green improves the more you play to the right. You will want a good angle into this green because it is modeled after the twelfth at the Old Course at St. Andrews, a hole that is much admired by the Spanish Bay design triumvirate. The green is sharply plateaued, in the shape of a top hat, with a flat putting surface that drops off on all sides just like, well, a top hat. "It might be controversial because it is so abrupt, but I like it," Watson says, "The concept is that, if you can put a shot up on top the flat portion of the green, you will have an easy birdie chance."

The thirteenth is a tiny par three, inspired by the Postage Stamp hole at Troon in Scotland, which looks to be equally dangerous, at least for the weekend player. The green is angled into the side of a dune, and marks the return of the course to the linksland holes. The fourteenth is an absolutely glorious par five that plunges straight for the sea as if impatient for a return to the promised land. One has a sense of great exuberance playing down its wide, undulating fairway even though it is very long and surrounded by the shaggy, windswept wilderness.

Much of the site, particularly near the ocean, has been left in its

The long seventeenth, running hard beside the sea, allows us to glimpse nature's rough-hewn beauty before taking on its raw challenges, which is linksland golf at its best.

natural state, a habitat for tall sea grasses, ice plant, thick clumps of creeping shrubs and other species of plants and animals. By edict, these cannot be disturbed. This was a condition imposed by the California Coastal Commission when it allowed the resort to be built. Some of these habitats had to be skirted in the design, and signs are posted about the course warning golfers of dire consequences should they be discovered wandering about in the forbidden territory. At the fifteenth hole, for example, one of these habitats cuts across the fairway, forcing a lay up off the tee. This cannot be seen from the tee because a large bunker obscures the view of the landing area. Forewarned is forearmed, then, because the second shot is a crackerjack with a forced carry across the wasteland past an array of bunkers to a green that curls around the edge of a small, bunkered dune. When the flag is tucked around the back, behind the bunker, it appears unassailable. The ground in front is shaped into fetching little hollows and mounds designed to toss aside a weak approach, yet the green will gather certain shots and send them 'round the bend to the hole. It's a provocative little hole with a nice sting in its tail.

After a stout one-shotter at the sixteenth, with its green folded into a hollow beside the beach, one arrives at the seventeenth and, surely, pauses long enough to take in the view. It is a scene straight out of the last century, with the slightly faded colors of the turf and wild grasses turning to a rich glow under the slanting rays of the sun. One can almost see one of those old characters from a Douglas Grant painting, flailing away with a sand-pitted cleek as the wind turns his knuckles raw. The seventeenth plays alongside the ocean for its entire length, 414 yards, its fairway island little more than patches stuck onto the turbulent landscape. The hole clambers over the dunes, turning gradually to the right toward the ocean where the green hovers above the tangled wasteland that closes in on three sides. The approach will normally be played with a long club, into the wind, and there is ample incentive to summon your best stroke because a deep, dish-like swale sprawl across the front of the green ready to cast your shot into oblivion. Abandon all hope, ye who enter.

The eighteenth is a rough and rugged finishing hole, a par five which looks to be long enough, at 571 yards, and tough enough to breed respect. The way these brutes are playing the game nowadays, though, I am sure to be proven wrong. They will undoubtedly be ripping it home in two shots, with scarcely a blink, but the ordinary player will not often reach it in two. The hole is shaped around to the left but is designed to be attacked, if that is the word, by a straight shot, or even a slight fade. One plays from fairway island to fairway island, fighting the instinct to go left where all of one's power and most of the trouble lie. The finish, though not as visually satisfying as one hoped for, is as formidable as one wants to see. Beginning about a half mile or so from the green is a center bunkering structure of gargantuan proportions that rises to a plateau with a tiny sliver of fairway on top. At the end of this is the green, surrounding which is a grisly marshland hazard that is a tangle of unyielding sedge grasses and gnarled bushes. Here and there lie the bleached remains of cypress limbs, looking like so many twisted bones abandoned in the wilderness.

This macabre symbolism might appeal to the cheerful Scots, dismal lot that we are, but we will not end on so somber a note. Whether or not this golf course will become, as I think it will, one of America's great ones is a matter that time, maintenance and future

The tiny thirteenth, modeled after the 'Postage Stamp' hole at Troon in Scotland, is angled into the side of a dune that rises on the left and falls away steeply to the right.

opinion will decide. For me, it is enough that Jones and Watson and Tatum have combined their considerable knowledge and particular talent to give us an authentic linksland course of such beauty and interest. They have poured much of themselves into this project, their attitudes toward the game, their feelings for links golf, the values they cherish, and I have the impression that most of it is there on the ground, where happily, anyone can experience and play it. If you are in any doubt as to what you find, listen to the conscience of the course, Sandy Tatum: "My feelings for links golf began when I was a student in England. Every weekend we played matches and not once was a match canceled because of weather. I learned that golf was marvelous fun if you just took the elements as they were, put on some heavy gear and decided to have at it. That experience left a deep impression on me. I love the game when you have to think your way around the golf course, where you play the ball down into the wind if that's the sensible thing to do, where you have access to the greens on the ground, where you accept bad bounces. This is so different from the game that evolved in this country, which is played mostly in the air, to relatively receptive greens, it doesn't make much difference where you're playing the shot from. This course is the realization of a dream for all of us. For me, it was an opportunity to be involved in something I care about deeply. It still gives me goose bumps. Bobby Jones has been working on this course for ten years. Every golf architect in the country knew about the property and all were keenly interested. Bobby has strong environmental credentials, which turned out to be a critical element in this project, and I know how he felt when it was awarded to our team. And Tom Watson didn't surprise me, because I know how thoughtful he is and how passionate he is, and all of that came bursting through. It was wonderful to see, and to work with." The lone disappointment is that there is no practice range at Spanish Bay. One somehow feels that a course like this should have one.

And what of that hardy band of earlier golfers, and those who have followed them across the linksland of Scotland? Would they like Spanish Bay, I wonder? I think you can put it this way. If you were to offer a Scotsman the choice of playing Spanish Bay or a free bottle of whiskey, he would think about it.

The fifteenth is a provocative par four that plays across the wasteland to a green that curls around a bunkered dune.

A closeup of the green is shown on pages 138—139, with fetching hollows and mounds in front and a shallow swale invading the green on the left.

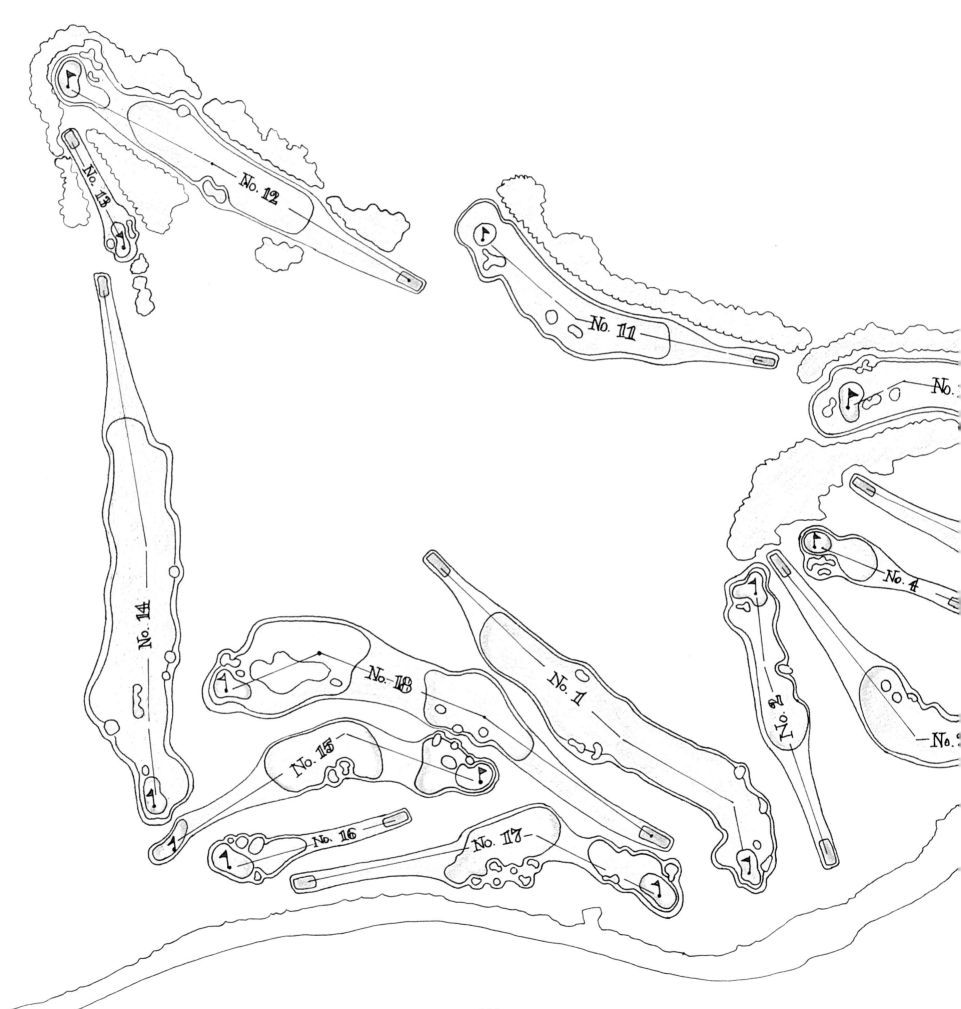

THE LINKS AT SPANISH BAY

COURSE RATING: 74.7

HOLE	1	2	3	4	5	6	7	8	9		10	11	12	13	14	15	16	17	18		
PAR	5	4	4	3	4	4	4	3	4	35	5	4	4	3	5	4	3	4	5	37	72
YARDS	500	307	405	190	459	395	418	163	394	3,231	520	365	432	126	571	390	200	414	571	3,589	6,820

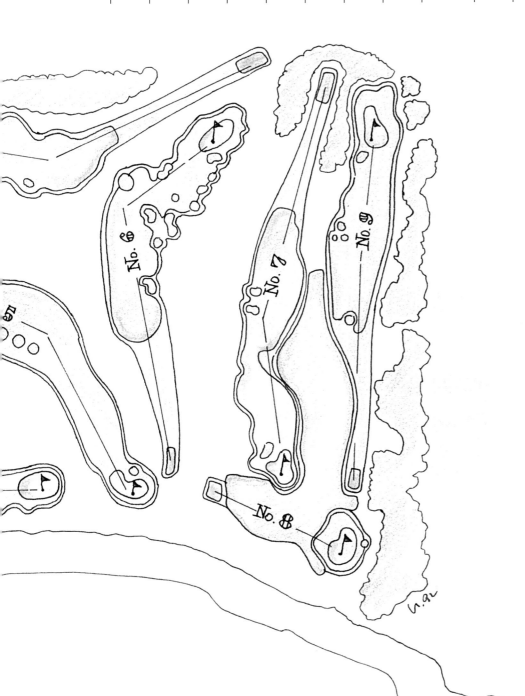

ROBERT TRENT JONES, JR., TOM WATSON AND SANDY TATUM,
GOLF ARCHITECTS

Pacific Grove Golf Links

*T*HE OLDEST GOLF COURSE AT the Monterey Peninsula was not actually built on the Monterey Peninsula. It was placed at the site of the old Del Monte Hotel, just off the peninsula and east of the present Highway 68. Nine holes were laid out in 1897 by Charles Maud, a cheerful Brit who was a polo enthusiast and an amateur golfer. Maud had designed California's first golf course in 1892 at a place called Pedley Farms in Arlington, a course that has been substantially revised and is now known as Victoria Golf Club. Maud was a man of firsts, California's first state amateur champion and the first president of the Southern California Golf Association. Maud's layout at Del Monte was revised and another nine were added by W. Herbert Fowler in 1920. Fowler was then considered one of the three or four best golf architects that England had produced, a reputation that persists today. His

design of Walton Heath, in the heathlands south of London, and his later remodeling of famous links such as Westward Ho! would have a wide influence on golf architecture. Over the years, the old Del Monte course has been altered several times in response to the inevitable pressure of commercial development, and a few of Fowler's holes remain as they were. Nevertheless, there are touches of the old master here and there. It is one of those relatively simple courses where the game can be taken at one's leisure.

It is fairly flat and short, with tight fairways and small greens, with pleasing reminders of an older style of golf architecture. Its hazards are not penal and therefore it can be played in a relatively short time, a virtue shared by few modern courses. The Del Monte course, once part of an exclusive resort playground, is now operated as a public course by the Pebble Beach

Company. From the beginning Sam Morse seems to have shown an interest in providing public golf as a part of the recreational mix he was creating. We can be glad that he did, because it led to the establishment of a municipal course at the northern tip of the Monterey Peninsula that is one of those delightful surprises you come upon from time to time.

The Pacific Grove Golf Links is situated just outside the Del Monte Forest at a place called Point Piños. Morse had sold this property to the municipality of Pacific Grove very early on, for $10,000, with stipulation that it remain forever open space. He urged that the town build a municipal golf course, and recommended as the designer Chandler Egan, the man who had so impressed Morse with his changes to the Pebble Beach course a few years earlier. The first nine holes of the Pacific Grove course, designed by Egan, were opened in 1932. Eventually, another nine holes would be added by Jack Neville, the original designer of Pebble Beach. Egan's nine travel over inland terrain and capture much of the charm of an English rural course done in the old style. There was once a railroad track running through the front nine, not an especially welcome feature, but then railroads were sometimes found near the older courses in Great Britain. The second nine, which opened in 1960, are laid out in dunesland that approaches the sea. Overlooking the course is a lighthouse, built 130 years ago, a sentinel that is no longer in use but now stands as a picturesque landmark for the course.

The course is as plain and natural as a village links in Ireland. The holes are unpretentious, reminiscent of an era when the par fours were sometimes less than 300 yards and the par threes could be contemplated with comfort by the common folk. There are not many bunkers, and the greens are small. The holes among the dunes are rugged and simple, but full of interest. Away from the fairways lie untamed, grassy dunes and sticky ice plant, which supply all of the difficulty one wants on so charming a course. There is just enough peril to whet the appetite. The fairways contain a good deal of kikuyu grass, which when properly tended and mowed, provides a good playing surface. The turf is sturdy and the ball tends to sit up, although you won't want to take much of a divot because the tough kikuyu turf will seize the club and end the stroke suddenly.

The Pacific Grove Links is the

The opening page shows the par five twelfth hole which swings around the boiling dunes alongside the ocean.

kind of place to take a Sunday bag to, so that you may play along at an unhurried pace that allows a full appreciation of the natural surroundings. As one might expect, Pacific Grove is a very popular course. It operates from a plain wooden clubhouse, built in 1961, that is adequately supplied with a pro shop and eating facilities. The starter, an amiable man named Finley Freedle, reports that more than seventy thousand rounds of golf are played here each year, an average of about two hundred per day. There is a group of twenty to thirty players, known as the 'Two O'Clock Gang,' that plays nine holes every day. They start at two o'clock on weekdays because they are all working men; on weekends, they have been known to play all day. Apparently, bad weather is the only thing that will stop this determined band of golfers, and when it does, I wonder what they would say to the Olde Golfer. "Rain is a blessing," said the Olde Golfer. "It gives the golfer an opportunity to meet his family." The course is open every day but Christmas. There is a large sign in the pro shop that announces, "A set of clubs and a golf bag is mandatory for all players when plying this course—by Order of the City of Pacific Grove," an indication, at least, of

how appealing it might be to stroll the course with only three or four clubs, stopping now and again to play a stroke. There is, however, ample space on the grounds for walking and picnicking. The lighthouse is now operated as a tourist attraction, and can be explored at ones leisure.

There is such a wonderful sense of playing golf on a simpler and entirely satisfying level that I wonder why this course isn't more widely known. I suppose that it cannot compete with the dramatic wonders of the other Monterey Peninsula courses, but the Pacific Grove course is a wonder all its own. It is unassuming and playful and very natural, qualities we do not always encounter and sometimes miss on modern golf courses. When the Pacific Grove Links opened in 1932, the green fee for nine holes was 25 cents. Today, the fee is $15 for nine holes, $25 for eighteen holes—a little more on weekends. Times have changed, haven't they? But this lovely little golf course has not, and that is something for which we can be very grateful.

The dunes holes play back and forth below the picturesque lighthouse, a Pacific Grove landmark. To the right, a view across the thirteenth green toward the fourteenth tee.

Above, the Old World charm of the inland holes is visible at the third hole, just 302 yards in length.

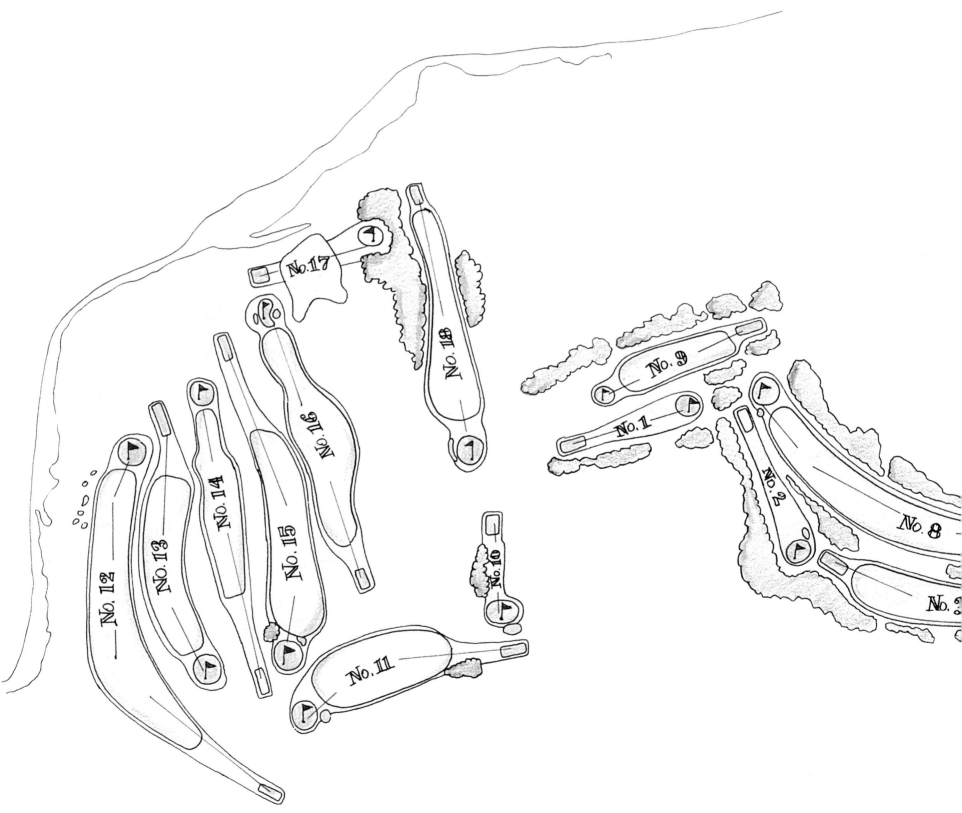

PACIFIC GROVE GOLF LINKS

COURSE RATING: 66.3

HOLE	1	2	3	4	5	6	7	8	9		10	11	12	13	14	15	16	17	18		
PAR	3	3	4	4	5	5	4	4	3	35	3	4	5	4	4	4	4	3	4	35	70
YARDS	143	194	302	258	511	524	302	410	215	2,859	102	280	500	301	345	385	353	136	292	2,694	5,553

JACK NEVILLE, GOLF ARCHITECT

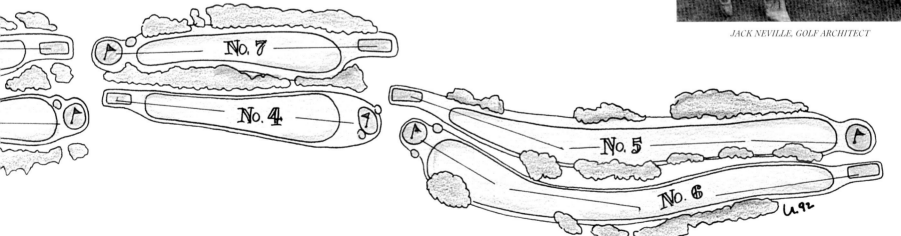

Credits

Golf course photographs by Udo Machat

ADDITIONAL PHOTOGRAPHY:
Pages 6, 123, 152, 153, 156, courtesy Pebble Beach Company
Page 38, courtesy Ralph W. Miller Golf Library
Pages 103, 145, courtesy Robert Trent Jones, Jr.
Page 59, courtesy Robert Trent Jones

Acknowledgments

Those who have given aid and comfort to the author include many who have shared their personal recollections and others who have helped to sort out historical facts from myths. All of these good people are collaborators, in one way or another, and their generosity is appreciated.

For significant contributions, I am deeply indebted to Lewis Lapham, Byron Nelson, Sandy Tatum, Bob Hanna, Ken Venturi, Hank Ketcham, Cary Middlecoff, Harvie Ward, Charles Seaver, Henry Puget and Robert Trent Jones, Jr. For much of the flavor and lore, I thank Mike Souchak, Phil Harris, Bob Rosburg, Frank Thacker, Dave Marr, Warner Keeley, F.A. 'Buck' Henneken, Jack Burke, Jr., George Coleman, Ed Sneed, Art Bell, Bob Sommers and Nelson Cullenward. For other valuable help I am grateful to Robert Trent Jones, Fran Hannigan, John Fleming, Tom Watson, Bill Spence, Ron Whitten, Art Spander, Denise St. Jean, and the late Jean Bryant at the Ralph W. Miller Golf Library.

For their many courtesies and invaluable asistance I thank Richard Maynes, John Zoller, Pierson Plummer, Carol Rissel, Cliff Coleman, Jack Guio, Dennis Bryan, Bill and Nancy Borland, Fran Teal, Bob Holmes and Karen Hunter along with her staff at Pebble Beach Company. Also, I want to acknowledge historical researcher Elmer Lagorio for uncovering several fascinating architectural clues and for checking many historical facts.

And finally, for her initial help and encouragement, a very special thanks to Carol Anne Swenson.

SAMUEL F.B. MORSE